EMPLOYEE STOCK OPTIONS

A Strategic Planning Guide
for the 21st Century Optionaire

GABRIEL FENTON

JOSEPH S. STERN, III

MICHAEL GRAY, CPA

STILLMAN PUBLISHING

Stillman Publishing
2740 Greenwich St., Suite 519
San Francisco, California 94123
Stillmanpublishing@hotmail.com

First printed in April 2000

10 9 8 7 6 5 4 3 2 1

Manufactured in the United States of America

Publisher's Cataloging-in-Publication
(Provided by Quality Books, Inc.)

Fenton, Gabriel.
    Employee stock options : a strategic planning
guide for the 21st century optionaire / Gabriel
Fenton, Joseph S. Stern, III, Michael Gray. -- 1st ed.
        p. cm.
        LCCN: 00-100758
        ISBN: 0-9678668-0-4 (hbk.)
        ISBN: 0-9678668-1-2 (pbk.)

    1. Employee stock options. 2. Investments.
I. Stern, Joseph S. II. Gray, Michael.
III. Title.

HD4928.S74F46 2000   658.3'225
                          QBI00-247

Dedication

to my wife, Jamie

Without your support, this book would still be a dream.
Thank you for making so many of my dreams come true.

Gabriel

ACKNOWLEDGMENTS

We would like to thank the following people who have helped in a myriad of ways in the preparation and writing of this book.

First, the Coles, the "original optionaires" and the motivation for this book.

William Prescott, the words behind the ideas, it was a pleasure working with you.

Brad Masterson, all your legwork in the publishing of this book is deserving of a new pair of shoes.

Jeff Kirkendall, CPA, and Heather Hall, CPA, thank you for your comments and contributions.

Ira Silver, Ph.D., over the years, your technical advice and mathematical skills have been critical.

Sandy and Peter Stern, you have always been there and supported me on everything I have ever done.

Dr. John LeRoy, thank you for taking the time to review the concept and encouraging the completion of the project.

Joseph S. Stern, Jr., you have been my biggest inspiration in life.

Robert Pastore, CPA, CFA, you were instrumental in laying the groundwork for this book.

Kurt Bauer, your enthusiasm was encouraging and helped spur the book along.

Stefan Lai, meeting you helped facilitate the idea of writing the book.

Attorney Stefan Fenton, the real author of the Fenton household, thank you for all your assistance.

Patrick and Michael Starzan, I truly appreciate your always being "on call."

Finally, to all our clients at Intel, Cisco, Lucent and many other technology companies across the country who are working on redesigning how we live with new technology, thank you for your support (and please hurry up and increase our modem speed).

DISCLAIMER

EMPLOYEE STOCK OPTIONS: A Strategic Planning Guide for the 21st Century Optionaire is intended for a wide audience with varying degrees of investment and option experience. Each person who reads this book will have a unique financial position, different financial goals, and a distinct income tax situation. This book should not be relied upon as a stand-alone document. Each reader's own investment and tax planning needs must be analyzed by a qualified professional.

Throughout the book, hypothetical examples are frequently used. These examples do not represent, and are not intended to represent, real people, real situations, or actual advice on particular stocks or option strategies. Although they are meant to be realistic, the examples used are for illustrative purposes only.

The option strategies outlined in this book involve risk and are not suitable for everyone. Prior to entering into any option contract, a person must carefully review a copy of *Characteristics and Risks of Standardized Options*; a prospectus is available from The Options Clearing Corporation. In addition, your brokerage firm can provide you with this material. An investor considering investing in options should consult with a tax advisor regarding how taxes may affect the outcome of their option transactions.

In writing this book, every effort was made to ensure an error-free document. Nonetheless, it is possible that the book may contain typographical or even content mistakes. The material in the text is based upon securities and tax laws in effect at the time of the writing. That laws change frequently is all the more reason you should speak with an advisor prior to making tax or investment decisions in the areas addressed by this book.

Although the authors worked on this book as a collaborative effort, the investment strategy information is entirely the work of Messrs. Stern and Fenton, and the tax information is entirely the work of Michael Gray, CPA. Neither Gabriel Fenton nor Joseph S. Stern, III contributed any portion of the tax information.

Michael Gray did not contribute any portion of the investment strategy information.

The authors and Stillman Publishing shall not be liable or responsible to anyone for any loss or damage caused, or alleged to be caused, either indirectly or directly from the information contained herein.

If you are unwilling to be bound by this disclaimer, you may return the book within ten days of the book's purchase date for a full refund of the purchase price of the book. For instructions on how to receive your refund, please e-mail: StillmanPublishing@hotmail.com.

CONTENTS

INTRODUCTION

▼

You finally did it. After enduring late nights, long weekends, and difficult working conditions, your dream has come true. You're a millionaire—at least on paper. Your company has rewarded you with substantial holdings in company stock and stock options. With your fortune comes a net worth with two commas and the ability to buy a new car without negotiating terms. Maybe you're looking for a new home. Probably, you plan to retire early and be free during the years your parents thought of as their prime.

Congratulations. You are an ascendant example of the new economy. You have joined the ranks of those who have made fortunes in their company's stock and stock options. You are a 21st century optionaire.

In 1996, sixty-two high-tech millionaires were being created every hour, more than half a million that year. By 1999, eight hundred publicly traded companies were giving six million employees company stock options. And that figure does not even reflect the more traditional grants of stock and options to executives.

But for every flashy story of a new net millionaire, there are numerous untold tragedies. The same optimism that leads to success often leads to a downfall. The employees' faith in their own abilities, combined with their emotional investment in their companies' prospects, sometimes causes them to leave their assets unprotected.

Let us tell you a story. Not long ago, we met with a former senior software engineer of a company we will call StrikeItRich.com. His is a familiar story to us. He was originally granted 100,000 employee stock options, of which 40,000 were vested Incentive Stock Options (ISOs) and 60,000 were Non-Qualified Stock Options (NQSOs) with an exercise price of $1 per share.

StrikeItRich.com had its Initial Public Offering (IPO) in June

1997, at a price of $10 per share, and closed that day at $93.13. While the stock fluctuated in and out of the $90 trading range for the next several months, the new optionaire remained optimistic about the prospects for his company and did nothing to hedge the downside risk of his concentrated position. In the interim, his wife became pregnant with their first child and they began looking for a starter house for $700,000 in Silicon Valley. Their paper net worth from the employee stock options was roughly $9,000,000.

In March 1998, StrikeItRich.com released earnings at $.27 under Wall Street analysts' estimates. It turned out that they had a severe flaw in their distribution unit, which many analysts believed to be detrimental to their future growth potential. Several well-known brokerage houses downgraded the stock to a "Sell," and over the next few weeks, the company fell to $2 per share. The engineer's fortune had virtually disappeared in just a few weeks.

As the year progressed, and the distribution problems persisted, the engineer lost his job. He was forced to exercise his grant of 40,000 ISOs and 60,000 NQSOs within 30 days of his termination. He reluctantly exercised and sold a portion of his shares to cover the cost of the exercise and held the remaining stock in a last hope that the stock would recover. While this was going on, the engineer made his tax payment, but overlooked the Alternative Minimum Tax (AMT). By the time this oversight was recognized, the AMT due was substantially more than he had planned. To make matters worse, he had already taken out a margin loan and made a down payment on his new home. With no cash on hand and StrikeItRich.com's share price falling, the engineer had to file for bankruptcy.

All of this could have easily been avoided by applying the strategies we will reveal in the following chapters. If the engineer had come to us in time, we would have armed him with protective financial strategies, including the use of put options, portfolio diversification, and prudent tax-avoidance strategies. His company's stock would still have gone down, but he would not have crashed and burned with it.

In our work as investment advisors and derivative options specialists, we hear stories like this all too often. Optionaires are typically not experts in financial management. A certain heady feeling of invulnerability sometimes comes with sudden wealth. It's hard for optionaires to believe that the impressive intellectual capital of their companies could fail to negotiate the vagaries of the market. In short, optionaires often gamble without understanding the rules of the game.

Our job is to provide prudent strategies to stabilize the wild roller coaster ride that company stock and stock options often bring. We will cover many of these strategies in the following chapters. However, we must caution the reader that these approaches are not band-aids. They require a willingness to grasp financial realities about which optionaires are often uninformed.

After years of advising clients with these kinds of substantial holdings, we have observed that new optionaires usually wake to find themselves in an overwhelmingly complex position. With millions of dollars of paper net worth tied up in their companies' stock and options, their financial situation is fraught with many new dangers, such as:

1. the possibility of paying several times their salary in taxes
2. having their net worth fluctuate thousands to hundreds of thousands of dollars
3. a highly concentrated employee stock and option position, often comprising 70-90% of their liquid net worth
4. an income that has no real value, when compared to the value of their employee stock and options position

Yet for each of these common problems, there are viable solutions. Our purpose here is not to scare you. It is certainly not to uncover any "secret formula" for beating the employee stock option planning game (there is none). Our goal is to show you sophisticated and proven strategies to help you maximize your employee stock and stock options.

FOUR CORE PRINCIPLES

We think of the work that we do as helping individuals to turn their distinctive financial situations into real and lasting wealth. After years in this business, we have distilled our understanding of what it takes to turn a large company stock and options position into lasting affluence down to four core principles. They are:

1. **Realism**—being willing to admit that your stock may not grow faster than the broader market or even that it may not go up forever
2. **Advance planning**—having a strategy in place one to two years prior to taking action
3. **Hedging**—locking in your gains and deferring the tax liability
4. **Diversification**—reducing your risk. (There are other good investments aside from your company stock.)

All of the strategies you will learn flow from these principles. If you adhere to these fundamentals, not only will you be well on your way to financial freedom, you will also be able to sleep at night—without nightmares of a market collapse.

We have structured this book in a straightforward, easy-to-understand manner. Some sections, however, are unavoidably technical due to the complexity of the subject matter, and may only be appropriate for the experienced optionaire. Don't be afraid to skip these sections with the intent of seeking the aid of a qualified financial advisor. Read only the sections that you feel most comfortable with, but please do not become discouraged if you do not fully master every last detail. The book is not intended to be read cover to cover.

Our goals for our readers are similarly practical. When you have completed the book, you will be able to:

1. identify and understand what type of employee stock and options you have
2. determine when you should consider exercising your options
3. understand what strategies and actions you should employ for your options

Additionally, you should be able to avoid making common errors, including:

1. exercising the "wrong" type of option, or exercising at an inopportune time
2. putting tax consequences in front of market conditions
3. not protecting your paper gains

We applaud you for your willingness to learn something new, especially something that can be so crucial to your future. We intend to make it as easy on you as possible. One of our motivations in writing this book comes from observing that some of our clients initially try to do their planning themselves, including educating themselves on all of the esoteric aspects of employee stock options. They quickly find themselves overwhelmed. These clients spend so much time trying to research the complexities of employee stock options and managing their investments that they take on, in effect, an extra job. We have found that our clients have more than enough work to do with one job, and should not try to moonlight as options gurus, just as we should not try to moonlight as software engineers. So we have created this book in order to make the fundamentals of these strategies accessible.

This book will enable you to intelligently discuss derivative options strategies with your investment advisor so that, together, you can make the right decisions. However, it should not be used as a substitute for a competent financial advisor. By competent, we mean experienced in these particular financial strategies. Most tax attorneys and investment advisors are not experts on this material. It is crucial to find an advisor who specializes in these areas. (See Conclusion: *Questions to Ask a Financial Advisor and Other Considerations*.)

FEAR AND GREED

One final cautionary note: Investor psychology is driven by two factors, fear and greed. We assume that if you had the daring to work in a pre-IPO company, or put in extra hours for stock in a major firm, fear is not your problem. But let us emphasize the importance of not being too greedy. Optionaires who apply dangerous strategies, such as leveraging their positions, often find themselves much worse off. It is a wonderful thing to accumulate a substantial amount of wealth in a relatively short period of time. Keep your personal finances and goals in perspective and you will be able to turn that short period into a much longer one.

Having witnessed the highs and lows of compensatory employee stock options, from overnight millionaires to financial disasters, we have concluded that it is one thing to be a millionaire on paper, and quite something else to sustain it. We hope that you will use our experience and knowledge to make the transition from the giddy heights of sudden wealth to lasting security and affluence. And so to you, the 21st Century Optionaire, we dedicate this book.

GETTING THE MOST
OUT OF THE BOOK

This book is designed to be used as a reference guide and is not intended to be read cover to cover. Use the Table of Contents to guide you to the sections which are most relevant and useful to you.

Be sure to read through the Key Terms and Phrases first. You can also consult the Definitions at the end of the book.

The list of Frequently Asked Questions provides another summary of information.

Chapters 2, 3, 4, and 5 attempt to follow the optionaire's career cycle. We recognize that you may have entered the career cycle at differing levels, and given that people go through cycles of change throughout their careers, we encourage you to plan not only for today but for the future. Find the chapter that is most applicable to your current situation and read that and the following chapter in their entirety.

We do not expect that you will learn all of the intricacies and details of planning for your concentrated employee stock option position, but we hope you will conclude that working with a qualified financial advisor is a key element to increasing your net worth and reducing your tax implications. As much as we would love to share the golden bullet of tax reduction and profit explosion, there is not one simple answer.

ONE

▼

KEY TERMS
AND PHRASES

Following is a selection of key terms and phrases that you must understand before proceeding with this book. In addition to this section, there is a glossary at the end of the book that contains other commonly used terms and phrases.

ALTERNATIVE MINIMUM TAX (AMT)

The alternative minimum tax (AMT) was created so that taxpayers with substantial income would pay tax.

The federal income tax is actually a parallel tax system. There is a "regular" tax that most of us are fairly familiar with. There is also an "alternative minimum tax" (AMT). Your tax is computed using both methods, and you generally pay the higher tax. If the alternative minimum tax does apply, a portion of the excess over the regular tax may be available as a tax credit in a later year, treated somewhat like a prepayment of the later year's tax.

The alternative minimum tax rates are 26% for the first $175,000 of alternative minimum taxable income (AMTI) and 28% for AMTI over $175,000. The maximum rates as described above for the regular tax for sales of capital assets on or after January 1, 1998, will also apply for the alternative minimum tax. Single persons have an AMT exemption of $33,750, phased out by 25% of the excess of AMTI over $112,500, and eliminated for AMTI of $247,500 or more. The AMT exemption on a joint return for married persons is $45,000, phased out by 25% of the excess of AMTI over $150,000, and eliminated for AMTI of $330,000 or more.

DISQUALIFYING DISPOSITION

A disqualifying disposition is created when Incentive Stock Option (ISO) acquired stock is sold within two years of the option grant date and one year from the exercise date. This transaction is taxed as ordinary income.

EXERCISE PRICE / OPTION PRICE
STRIKE PRICE / GRANT PRICE

All of these terms refer to the price at which the holder of employee stock options is entitled to buy the underlying company stock. This price is used to determine the cost of exercising employee stock options and the amount of taxes due on an exercise.

EXPIRATION DATE

The expiration date is the date on which the right to exercise your employee stock options expires. All vested, non-exercised options will be lost after the expiration date.

GRANT DATE

The grant date is the specific day on which employee stock options are given to the employee from the employer.

INCENTIVE STOCK OPTION (ISO)

A type of employee stock option. ISOs are commonly referred to as qualified stock options, because they qualify for preferential tax treatment.

When ISOs are exercised, the optionaire does not recognize a taxable gain. Instead, the exercise increases the individual's Alternative Minimum Taxable Income (AMTI). After the required holding period, which is twelve months from the exercise date and two years from the grant date, the gain on the sale of the ISO stock is taxed as a long-term capital gain (qualified disposition). If the stock is sold before the required holding periods listed above, the AMTI is eliminated and the gain is treated as a disqualifying disposition and is taxed as ordinary income.

For an employee stock option to be an ISO, it must meet the following requirements:

1. The options must be granted with an exercise price equal to the current fair market value of the underlying stock.
2. The options can only be granted to employees of the issuing company. Thus, independent contractors, board members, etc., cannot receive ISOs.
3. The options cannot have a life of more than ten years.

INITIAL PUBLIC OFFERING (IPO)

The first time a company offers its shares for sale to the public on the open market.

LONG-TERM CAPITAL GAINS TAX

Under current tax law, when a security is purchased and held for twelve months or more, it qualifies for long-term capital gains. Currently, the long-term capital gains tax rate is 20%. (As with all tax laws, there are exceptions to this rule.)

NON-QUALIFIED STOCK OPTION (NQSO)

A type of employee stock option. As opposed to ISOs, NQSOs do not qualify for preferential tax treatment. When NQSOs are exercised, the optionaire is taxed on the gain as ordinary income and is subject to payroll tax withholding.

OPTION GRANT

The term refers to a specific group of employee stock options, ISOs or NQSOs, that are given to the employee by the employer. Grants are identified by their unique grant numbers.

When exercising employee stock options, it is essential that you inform the exercise administrator which grant of options are to be exercised for tax and financial planning purposes.

OPTIONAIRE

An individual who has accumulated substantial wealth through company stock and options.

VESTED OPTIONS

Vested options are options that have passed the required holding period, and can be exercised.

TWO

▼

PRE-IPO AND
POST-IPO PLANNING

JOHN GETS EATEN ALIVE BY AMT

John Baker graduated from college and then spent several years in a job that was good enough to pay the bills, but not much more. Tired of the day-to-day monotony with his current job, he began looking for a new position, specifically in the technology sector. While he had few technical skills, he pursued a job in marketing with a pre-IPO company in the networking industry.

It was more than a job. It was fourteen-hour days, cramped work conditions and endless pressure. John didn't take a day off for months at a time. He only communicated with his friends through email. He had terrible bags under his eyes, and most of the meals he ate were delivered.

But John knew his diligence was worth it. He excelled at his work and climbed his way up to a managerial position. By the time his company had announced that it was going public, John had accumulated a sizeable position of ISOs with a low exercise price. He had heard of a strategy by which you could exercise and hold your options before the company went public to minimize potential AMT liabilities, but was so busy that he did not take advantage of it.

Six months later, the company had their IPO and the stock came out at $19 per share. On the first day of trading, the stock doubled to $38 per share. At the time, he saw no point in exercising, thinking that he had missed his opportunity to exercise and hold his ISOs while the stock was trading at a low price. (The reason you may want to exercise and hold ISOs when the stock is at a lower price is the smaller the spread between the grant price and the market price, the less the potential AMT liability you face.) In hindsight, John was lucky he did not exercise and hold his ISOs, since he would have faced higher tax consequences, because the stock plummeted to $16 per share a month after the IPO.

Due to the pullback, John could now exercise his vested options and pay less AMT than if he had exercised when the stock was trading at $38 per share. We advised him to exercise and hold his ISOs, but once again, he got busy and did not act upon the suggestion. Then his luck ran out. A few months later, his company was bought out by a networking giant. The stock jumped up to $90 per share, and once again he had lost an excellent opportunity to exercise at a low price and reduce significant tax consequences.

In the end, John had to pay taxes that amounted to more than his income for the year. He was devastated. He had to sell stock to cover the taxes, an action that incurred even more tax. This is a classic example of a situation that could have been avoided with a little planning and strategic timing.

If John had exercised and held his options earlier or had taken advantage of the 83(b) Election, he would have put himself in a position to reduce his potential AMT liability as the stock price increased in value.

DON'T COUNT ON LUCK; COUNT ON PLANNING

So why does anyone put up with jobs as overwhelming as John's? The simple answer is stock options. Pre-IPO companies give stock options for one reason: to attract highly qualified, motivated individuals. As a pre-IPO employee, the number of options you receive may be ten times what you would have received at an established company.

With such intense work pressure, you probably believe that

you are too busy to research the benefits of your newly acquired stock options. We urge you to take the time to plan. In the long run, understanding your options may be as important to you as understanding your job. Many strategies exist that can help you to maximize your employee stock options.

For instance, most people think they are "handcuffed" to their employee stock options before their company goes public. This is not always true. You may be restricted from exercising and selling your options or hedging your position, but there are strategies that you can employ to minimize your tax liability and maximize your benefits.

HOW TO UNLOCK YOUR GOLDEN HANDCUFFS

ISOs and NQSOs, 83(b) elections, pre-IPO stock purchases, hedging, and the 180-day lockout period. As you receive your employee stock options, we highly recommend that you familiarize yourself with these terms and the related issues outlined below. Understanding them can allow you to maneuver financially in ways that may surprise you. When you discuss these approaches with your financial advisor, remember that there may be some variation in each situation, depending on your position in your company. For example, the more senior you are within your company, the more restrictions will likely be placed upon you by the company and the Securities Exchange Commission. Employ the following strategies, and you should be able to maximize your employee stock options and unlock the "handcuffs" that are seemingly restraining you.

EMPLOYEE STOCK OPTIONS

Employee stock options are probably the benefit with which you are least familiar. There are two types of options that you may receive as part of your compensation package: Incentive Stock

Options (ISOs) and Non-Qualified Stock Options (NQSOs). The primary difference between the two is that ISOs can offer a considerable tax benefit.

The advantage of ISOs over NQSOs is that when you exercise, you have the ability to exercise and hold your options without triggering an ordinary income tax. You are required to hold your shares for a minimum of twelve months from date of exercise and two years from the date of grant before qualifying for long-term capital gains treatment. Should you exercise and sell within twelve months from the exercise date and two years from the grant date, you will create a disqualifying disposition and will be taxed as ordinary income tax, similar to NQSOs. The downside of ISOs is that they may trigger AMT. You should consult a tax expert to find out if your ISO exercise will create an AMT liability. For upper level managers, it is important to discuss any exercising or trading restrictions that may exist with your stock plan administrator. Most senior managers and all officers have trading restrictions.

When you exercise NQSOs, regardless of whether you exercise and hold, exercise and sell, or exercise and sell to cover, you will be taxed as ordinary income at the time of exercise. The effect of this is that your tax bracket will likely increase after exercising your NQSOs. Typically, you will attempt to exercise NQSOs when the stock is trading at a high price, in order maximize your profit. On average, individuals exercising NQSOs will pay 45-50% ordinary income tax on their gain. This amount is withheld by the brokerage firm, so do not be surprised if the check that you receive for the proceeds is about half of what you expected.

When building a strategy to unwind your option position, please take a systematic approach. We highly recommended that you work with a qualified financial advisor who specializes in employee stock options to help you establish a plan of action. This, above all, will help to take some of the emotion out of your decision-making process. Experience has shown that employees become emotionally attached to their company stock and are afraid to exercise, for fear that they will miss the next big increase in share price. (Refer to the *Emotional Intelligence Quiz* in the Appendix.) The inability to divorce emotional attachment to options from strategic decisions generally leads to two common errors:

1. waiting too long to exercise your ISOs, and selling your NQSOs too soon
2. deciding when to exercise based on tax consequences rather than market conditions

THINGS TO DO ONCE YOU RECEIVE YOUR GRANT OF STOCK OPTIONS

1. Build a file to maintain all the paperwork you receive about your employee stock options.
2. If your company does not provide you with a spreadsheet of your current stock option position, you should create your own. It should contain the following: grant number, option type (ISO or NQSO), number of options, grant date, expiration date, vesting date, options vested, and options exercised. (See the *Employee Stock Option Worksheet* in the Appendix.)
3. Speak with your Human Resources department or stock plan administrator to ensure that you understand the specific details of your option grant. Make sure to inquire about trading and derivative restrictions.
4. Before exercising your options you should speak with a tax consultant to find out about tax implications of exercising options and speak with a financial advisor to make sure that your exercise strategy is appropriate.

83(B) ELECTION
Possibly one of the most overlooked benefits that may be available to the pre-IPO company, the 83(b) election can potentially

offer a good deal of tax planning freedom in exercising your options. It does not apply in all cases, so you should consult your stock plan administrator once you receive your option grant.

Historically, option plans did not allow the optionee to exercise non-vested options. More recently, however, many companies have changed their policy. The advantage of doing this depends mainly on the fair market value of the shares at the time of exercise. Remember, ISOs must be granted with an exercise price equal to the fair market value of the underlying shares. If the option holder exercised the options on the same day the options are granted, the income recognized for AMT purposes would be zero. (Remember that AMTI is equal to the difference between the fair market value of the shares at the date of exercise and the exercise price.) Additionally, the holding period for long-term capital gains would begin at the date of exercise. The disadvantage of this approach is that the holder must buy the shares and thus make a cash investment in the company. This strategy is very effective for start-up companies that have low stock values.

One crucial thing to keep in mind before exercising your options, pre-IPO, is that you may lose any money that you paid for the exercise and your shares may be worthless, if your company does not go public or is not acquired. Rules differ and we recommend that you speak with your company. This may be a gamble in some cases, so if you feel that your cost is high, you will want to make certain that you can afford the monetary loss or that you do not plan on leaving your company in the near future.

To obtain the benefits described above, the holder must file an election with the Internal Revenue Service under Section 83(b) of the Internal Revenue Code. The election allows the holder to recognize all of the tax consequences related to the exercise of the options as of the date of exercise. This is important because, by doing this, the holder locks in the low fair market value for AMT purposes. If a holder early exercised options but did not make the 83(b) election, AMTI would not be recognized until the options vested and the income would be measured based on the values at the date of vesting, not the date of exercise. This difference could be substantial if the company's stock value increases significantly due an IPO or some other transaction.

The 83(b) election is required even when the income amount is zero and must be made within 30 days after exercising the option. The election is made by filing a written statement to the Internal Revenue Service office where the taxpayer files his or her income tax return. A copy of the election statement is also attached to the income tax return for the date of exercise.

THE EMPLOYEE STOCK PURCHASE PLAN (ESPP)

Aside from granting you employee stock options as an incentive bonus, your employer may also allow you to purchase company stock through the Employee Stock Purchase Plan (ESPP). Through ESPP you will be able to contribute a specified percentage of your income to purchase company stock. In certain instances, many companies allow their employees to purchase company stock at a discount. The larger the discount to the share price, the more sense it makes to contribute to your ESPP. Most employees who are bullish on the company choose to participate in ESPP.

You should confer with your Human Resources department or stock plan administrator for the details of your company's ESPP. Issues to discuss include:

1. What is the maximum contribution you can make to your ESPP?
2. Can you purchase company stock at a discount?
3. Does the company match your contribution?
4. Is there a vesting period for stock that you purchase through the ESPP?

HEDGING YOUR POSITION AFTER THE IPO

Jane has worked for a recent IPO data storage company for the past two years. When the company went public, she had a position of 50,000 ISOs. Jane refused to hedge her position as the price of her company stock had tripled from its IPO price of $20 per share to $60 per share in three months. She could not see the stock price falling after such a robust start and did not want to pay the premium to hedge her position and lock in her gains. Jane was a gambler and she lost the bet. With a paper net worth of approximately $3,000,000, the data storage market collapsed and her company's stock dropped to $8 per share. The stock was deemed highly overvalued and to this date has not recovered.

We believe that this kind of loss may happen more often than not. One recent study found that nine out of ten companies' share value will drop below its original IPO price within twelve months. Because of this, we highly recommend that you take the necessary precautions to avoid becoming victim to this statistic.

During the pre-IPO period, you will be unable to directly hedge your position. That is to say, you cannot use derivatives, such as puts and calls, of your own company to lock in gains or reduce downside risk. The reason is simply that your companies' stock is not trading on an exchange and in turn does not have listed options. Until your company goes public, you will have to resort to alternative methods.

A plausible way to reduce the overall risk of having a concentrated position is by hedging against an index within your industry group. For example, if you work within the Internet sector, you can buy a put on an Internet index as a substitute. While this will not guarantee a one-for-one price hedge on downside risk, it is a viable alternative.

THE 180-DAY LOCKOUT PERIOD

The lockout period begins when your company goes public

and typically lasts for 180 days from the IPO date. During this time, you may be restricted from using hedging strategies and exercising and selling your options to limit stock price fluctuations. However you are not restricted from developing a plan of action.

In the short term, you need to become educated about your new situation. You should consult your stock plan administrator to find out what the specific guidelines are for your employee stock options and if there are any restrictions involved. Upper management and corporate officers will need to pay special attention to company and Securities Exchange Commission (SEC) regulations.

In the long term, you should develop a systematic approach to unwinding your concentrated stock and option position with the goal of diversifying your assets. Believe it or not, there are companies out there whose stock may perform better than yours in the long run! To make qualified decisions on when to exercise, you must first develop a financial plan. Any good plan is based on realistic objectives that arise from answering the following questions. We suggest you put your answers down on paper, show them to your financial advisor, and review them annually.

STEPS TO BUILDING YOUR FINANCIAL PLAN

PERSONAL FINANCIAL GOALS

1. What are your goals and objectives, both personally and financially? For example:
    • first or second home, remodeling, mortgage
    • retirement or early retirement
    • children's education
    • investments, estate tax planning, insurance
2. How much risk do you want to take? Quantifying this answer can be difficult. We suggest that you

focus on your goals and the required total return needed to reach these goals.

3. What are your goals for the following time frames?
    • short-term (1-2 years)
    • mid-term (3-5 years)
    • long-term (5+ years)

CAREER AND FINANCIAL PLANNING

4. How long do you plan on staying with your company?
5. How bullish are you on your company's outlook, both short and long term?
6. What is the outlook for your sector?
7. Are you working with a financial advisor and/or tax advisor who specializes in employee options?

YOUR COMPANY STOCK AND OPTIONS

8. If your company is pre-IPO, have you considered taking advantage of the 83(b) election?
9. Do you plan on purchasing stock in your Stock Purchase Plan ESPP? If so, how much do you plan on contributing?
10. How much do you plan on contributing to your 401(k) plan?
11. How do you plan on investing your contributions?
    • percentage you plan on investing in the company stock
    • percentage you plan on investing outside company stock
12. How do you plan on exercising your stock options?
    • cashless exercise
    • exercise and sell to cover
    • exercise and hold

Once you have developed both a short- and long-term plan, you should feel comfortable knowing that you have accomplished the initial steps of the process. Now all you have to do is follow through with your plans. For optionaires who are overly attached to their company's stock and options, this can be the hardest part. Many individuals find it difficult to separate emotion from investing. (Refer to the *Emotional Intelligence Quiz* in the Appendix.)

IF YOU HOLD PRE-IPO OPTIONS

- Learn about the company and legal restrictions regarding your ISOs.
- Learn about 83(b) elections, and the potential AMT liabilities of exercising your ISOs after the IPO.
- Learn about hedging pre-IPO.
- Develop a strategic plan for exercising and holding your options, or participating in your ESPP, based on a carefully constructed, personal financial plan.

THREE

◆

NEW JOB AT AN
ESTABLISHED COMPANY

UMI GETS A GREAT JOB,
THEN FORGETS WHY

Umi Rathal graduated from M.I.T. on Sunday and started at Houston Systems on Monday. He was so excited that he could not contain himself. He was going to become an optionaire; there was no question in his mind. As he sat in the parking lot on that first morning at 6:15 a.m. waiting for the doors to open, he was excited to start working on the network design plans he would be implementing.

The next few days were a whirlwind of new faces, new names, and new systems. As the days turned into months, Umi continued to work intensively, and his company's share price continued to trend upwards. Umi was awarded ISOs and NQSOs. Through the blur of sixty- to eighty-hour work weeks, Umi realized that he was indeed on his way to becoming an optionaire.

One morning his manager interrupted his work schedule to say, "Umi, I want to review your progress over the past five years here at Houston Systems." "Five years?" thought Umi, "How is that possible? Where did the time go?"

Umi had lost track of a lot more than just time. He had lost track of his finances, and the benefits his company offered. Several crucial investment planning opportunities had slipped though his fingers. When he started work, he was given options, plus the right to partake in the company 401(k) and the Employee Stock

Purchase Plan (ESPP). As the years passed, Umi never bothered to sign up for these programs.

In general, we feel that everyone who can afford to save a portion of their salary should look into their company's 401(k) and ESPP. When Umi came to us, we were able to help him make a fresh start with his financial planning. Still, he had wasted years of precious time and financial advantages, because he was too busy doing his job to remember why he was doing it (to build a fortune).

DON'T LET IT HAPPEN TO YOU

Are you new to your company? As a new hire of an established company, there are a number of financial issues that you need to address immediately. They have to do with your employee compensation package. The complexity of your situation will vary, depending on your starting level and whether you are transferring from another company. Whatever situation you find yourself in, we recommend that you become familiar with the details of compensatory benefits, including your employee stock options, stock purchase plan, and 401(k) plan.

EMPLOYEE STOCK OPTIONS

Employee stock options are probably the benefit with which you are least familiar. There are two types of options that you may receive as part of your compensation package: Incentive Stock Options (ISOs) and Non-Qualified Stock Options (NQSOs). The primary difference between the two is that ISOs can offer a considerable tax benefit.

The advantage of ISOs over NQSOs is that when you exercise, you have the ability to exercise and hold your options without triggering an ordinary income tax. You are required to hold your shares for a minimum of twelve months from date of exercise and two years from the date of grant before qualifying for long-term capital gains treatment. Should you exercise and sell within twelve months from the exercise date and two years from the grant date, you will create a disqualifying disposition and will be taxed as ordinary income tax, similar to NQSOs. The downside of ISOs is that they may trigger AMT. You should consult a tax expert to find out if your ISO exercise will create an AMT liability. For upper level managers, it is important to discuss any exercising or trading restrictions that may exist with your stock plan administrator. Most senior managers and all officers have trading restrictions.

NQSOs are much more common at established companies, and are likely the type of option that you will be granted. When you exercise NQSOs, regardless of whether you exercise and hold, exercise and sell, or exercise and sell to cover, you will be taxed as ordinary income at the time of exercise. The effect of this is that your tax bracket will likely increase after exercising your NQSOs. Typically, you will attempt to exercise NQSOs when the stock is trading at a high price, in order maximize your profit. On average, individuals exercising NQSOs will pay 45-50% ordinary income tax on their gain. This amount is withheld by the brokerage firm, so do not be surprised if the check that you receive for the proceeds is about half of what you expected.

When building a strategy to unwind your option position, please take a systematic approach. We highly recommended that you work with a qualified financial advisor who specializes in employee stock options to help you establish a plan of action. This, above all, will help to take some of the emotion out of your decision-making process. Experience has shown that employees become emotionally attached to their company stock and are afraid to exercise, for fear that they will miss the next big increase in share price. (Refer to the *Emotional Intelligence Quiz* in the Appendix.) The inability to divorce emotional attachment to options from strategic decisions generally leads to two common errors:

1. waiting too long to exercise your ISOs, and selling your NQSOs too soon

2. deciding when to exercise based on tax consequences rather than market conditions

Things to do once you receive your grant of stock options:

1. Build a file to maintain all the paperwork you receive about your employee stock options.
2. If your company does not provide you with a spreadsheet of your current stock option position, you should create your own. It should contain the following: grant number, option type (ISO or NQSO), number of options, grant date, expiration date, vesting date, options vested, and options exercised. (See the *Employee Stock Option Worksheet* in the Appendix.)
3. Speak with your Human Resources department or stock plan administrator to ensure that you understand the specific details of your option grant. Make sure to inquire about trading and derivative restrictions.
4. Before exercising your options you should speak with a tax consultant to find out about tax implications of exercising options and speak with a financial advisor to make sure that your exercise strategy is appropriate.

EMPLOYEE STOCK PURCHASE PLAN (ESPP)

Aside from granting you employee stock options as an incentive bonus, your employer may also allow you to purchase company stock through the Employee Stock Purchase Plan (ESPP). Through ESPP you will be able to contribute a specified percentage of your income to purchase company stock. In certain instances, your company may even allow you to purchase company stock at a discount. The larger the discount to the share price, the more contributing to your ESPP makes sense. Most employees who are bullish on the company choose to participate in ESPP.

You should confer with your Human Resources department or

stock plan administrator for the details of your company's ESPP.
Issues to discuss include:

1. What is the maximum contribution you can make to
   your ESPP?
2. Can you purchase company stock at a discount?
3. Does the company match your contribution?
4. Is there a vesting period for stock that you purchase
   through the Employee Stock Purchase Plan?

401(K) PLAN

Another benefit that you will need to review is your 401(k)
plan. This is a retirement plan offered by most established companies, which allows you to contribute a percentage of your income
on a pre-tax basis and let the monies grow tax-deferred. Once
money is contributed to the plan, you cannot take distributions
until you reach the age of 59 1/2. If money is withdrawn prior to
this age, an early distribution penalty is assessed from the IRS.
When you take distributions, they will be taxed as ordinary income
on each dollar withdrawn. Some individuals will not want to take
distributions at age 59 1/2, and are not required to do so until age
70 1/2. (As with all IRS rules and regulations, there are exceptions.)

Your 401(k) plan is an excellent opportunity to begin diversifying your assets and receive a tax benefit. You will likely have
the ability to purchase company stock within your 401(k) plan as
well as a choice of mutual funds. It is important, however, to
maintain a good mix of investments within your portfolio.
Investment decisions should be based on your risk tolerance, as
well as your retirement income goals. A cautionary note: If you
choose to purchase company stock within your 401(k) plan, you
will further contribute to the over-weighting of your ownership
in your company stock, which increases your level of risk within
your portfolio.

If you are transferring from another company, you may have

had a 401(k) plan with your previous company. If this is the case, you can do one of three things:

1. Leave your account with your old company, if they allow you to.
2. Roll your account into your new company's 401(k) plan, if they allow you to.
3. Open a 401(k) IRA Rollover account with a brokerage firm and roll your money into this account.

The primary benefit of rolling your old 401(k) into your current company's 401(k) plan would be to have the ability to borrow against the account. (Not all companies allow you to do this.) If you see the ability to borrow as an important part of your overall financial plan, you may consider giving this further investigation.

The advantage of opening a 401(k) IRA Rollover account is that it will give you far greater investment choices versus the limited selection that you had with your old company or current one. You may decide to maintain a mutual fund portfolio or invest in stocks. Your investment decisions should be based on your current age, overall retirement goals, and risk tolerance. If you are nearing retirement, a more conservative and diversified approach may be more appropriate. Most importantly, if you are not comfortable making your own investment selections, do not just let the account remain undiversified.

As you can see, starting a new job with an established company involves many crucial financial issues. If you familiarize yourself with your newly acquired benefits, and build a systematic approach to maximize them, you will be on your way to a financially sound future.

Areas to look into:

1. vesting schedule for options
2. steps prior to exercise
3. pre-planning

IF YOU ARE A NEW HIRE AT AN ESTABLISHED COMPANY

- Familiarize yourself with all employee benefits, including stock options (ISOs and NQSOs), your 401(k) plan, and your Employee Stock Purchase Plan (ESPP).
- Take advantage of these benefits carefully, based on a well-developed understanding of your goals and risk tolerance.

FOUR

OLD PRO AT AN ESTABLISHED COMPANY

RAYMOND LOVED HIS COMPANY STOCK AND OPTIONS

At age thirty-four, Raymond was an old pro. He had moved through the ranks of his company, experiencing the IPO as employee number nine, watching his stock split four times, and becoming an optionaire many times over. During twelve years of hard work and spectacular success, Raymond had given little time to strategic option planning. Finally, he realized that it was time to get serious about his finances.

When we met with Raymond, he asked us, "Why should I diversify? If I had done that in years past, I would not be as rich today." This probably sounds familiar. For many people—and possibly you—there is a strong attachment to your company stock. After all, your company made you an optionaire; you understand its direction, and the direction of your industry. You probably feel confident that your company and its stock will continue to grow rapidly and outperform the broad markets.

DON'T LOVE YOUR STOCK AND OPTIONS TOO MUCH

We think loyalty and confidence are fine traits, as long as they do not cost you your fortune. Emotional attachment to financial vehicles can lead you to forego the rationality necessary to make some of the most important decisions you will ever make. That is what has happened to Raymond. He was conservative enough to stay with one company for twelve years, but with his own fortune he has been reckless. So far he has been lucky—his company's stock price remains high. But he has no guarantee that it will continue to do so. Raymond should probably have diversified and hedged his concentrated holdings long ago. Because he refused to consider this course of action, his attachment to his stock and options may undermine all that he has achieved.

Our message to you is: love your family, not your stock options. If you care for any financial vehicle too much, you are in danger of making financial decisions that are tainted with emotion. To make sure your approach is balanced, take this simple quiz:

EMOTIONAL INTELLIGENCE QUIZ

1. Have you ever felt that your company stock and option position was safe enough for you to ignore it for a period of time?
2. Have you ever felt that your stock and options were such a tremendous responsibility that you would rather just not think about them?
3. Have your company stock and options ever given you a feeling of power and/or invulnerability?
4. Has a dip in the price of your company stock ever made you feel depressed?
5. Do you feel comforted by your options?
6. Do you ever feel that your options look out for you?

If you answered yes to one or more of these questions, then it is likely that your financial decisions are somewhat distorted by emotion. A lack of objectivity in financial planning by optionaires usually leads to two kinds of crucial mistakes:

1. waiting too long to exercise options, with negative price and tax consequences
2. deciding to exercise based solely on tax consequences rather than on a combination of market conditions and tax consequences

Both of these mistakes can be disastrous. We recommend that anyone who has ever made emotional decisions about finance re-examine their attitudes towards their company stock and options. Be as honest and objective as possible. Imagine that the stock and options positions are not really yours, and that you are merely giving advice to someone else on preserving and growing their wealth. Take the following quiz:

OPTIONAIRE OBJECTIVITY QUIZ

1. Why am I holding a sizable percentage of my liquid assets in one investment?
2. Why do I feel my company will out-perform the broader market and the other companies within my industry?
3. Why do I feel my company will grow faster than our competitors' stock?
4. My peers, in the same financial situation, are also holding the bulk of their company options; do they know something I don't? What if their overweighting in their companies is correct and I'm wrong? What will happen to them if time demonstrates that I was right? What will happen to me if they are right?
5. Do I ever plan on selling a sizable percent of my company stock? When? Why then? Why not now?
6. How much money do I need? By when? How did I come to this amount?

7. What formula have I used to determine my tolerance to risk? Did I use a formula or did I just wing it?

Review your answers, be critical, and review them with your friends and family. If they feel that you are being too emotional, then you probably are and should seek the assistance of a financial advisor.

Your options do not require your love, but they do require your attention. We would never tell you that you are wrong about the outlook for your company's market performance. But we urge you to ask yourself, what if you are wrong? If you diversify your investment portfolio and your company stock continues to rise, you will not fully participate in the upside, but your portfolio should have less risk. However, if you are wrong and the price goes down, you may have only a fraction of the wealth you have today. Can you afford to lose the net worth you have vested in your options? We see it happen every day, and we can tell you objectively that the prudent step is almost always to diversify or hedge your position.

The first part of successful financial planning for the optionaire lies in objectivity about investing. The second part lies in objectivity about personal needs. Decisions are based on targeting objectives, and goals are based on needs.

OPTIONS STARTING TO EXPIRE

We have found that many people who have a tenure of five to ten years plus find themselves with blocks of expiring options that are deep in the money. This is a wonderful situation to be in, though it means you are about to give a substantial handout to your neediest relative, Uncle Sam.

Should options be exercised (held or sold) as soon as they vest, or should you wait until they are expiring? If you wait until they are near expiration, you will have to deal with the options that time, market conditions, and current tax laws have dealt you. By not planning, you give up control of your assets and future tax liabilities. The tax planning for expiring options pertains more for ISOs than NQSOs. This is due to the fact that taxes are triggered as soon as any exercise is made on NQSOs. For this reason, the following sections focus only on ISOs.

PROS OF EXERCISING AND HOLDING ISOs NOW

In general, we recommend exercising ISOs as they mature. We have four convincing reasons why:

1. **Minimizes AMT liability in the future**. If you feel confident that the share price will appreciate at a "good" pace in the future you should exercise and hold ISOs as soon as you can afford to do so. The smaller the spread on the exercise price versus the market price, the less the AMT liability.

2. **Minimizes capital gains tax**. Under current tax law ISOs held for more than twelve months qualify for long-term capital gains, 20%. The sooner you exercise and hold, the sooner you get the tax clock running.

3. **Uses the power of leverage**. Shares that you hold long can be used as collateral or margined; this can help finance tax payments, personal needs, the cost of exercising and holding ISOs, a down payment on a house, or other cash needs. Note that when one uses leverage in an investment they are increasing the amount of risk associated with the underlying asset. Do not use a leverage strategy without first consulting a qualified financial advisor and understanding the risk.

4. **Gives you control of your options**. Avoid option pileup. Option pile-up occurs when one has vested options expiring. At this point, time pressure plus

current market and tax conditions dictate your outcome and tax liability. Losing control of your
planning choices should be avoided at all cost.

CONS OF EXERCISING AND HOLDING ISOs

1. **Cash flow**: One must have cash to buy shares. This is
    equal to the Strike price multiplied by the number of
    shares you wish to exercise. Several of the larger bro-
    kerage firms will loan you the money to buy the
    shares, and you will pay interest to the brokerage
    firm in the form of a margin loan.
2. **Taxes**: Might trigger AMT, though you do not realize a
    gain or receive cash in hand at the time of the exercise.
3. **Opportunity cost**: Money spent on options could
    have been used for another investment or personal
    needs.
4. **Lack of diversification**: Potentially too much money
    in one investment.

CONSIDERATIONS IF YOU HAVE MORE NQSOs THAN ISOs

Like many old pros in dynamic companies, Raymond found
that not only had he neglected his financial planning for years, but
after many years at one company and several option exercises, he
had few ISOs remaining.

Remember NQSOs, unlike ISOs, are taxed at time of exercise
and are taxed as income. Often the exercise of NQSOs will place
the optionaire in the top federal income tax bracket of 39.6%, and
with a total tax liability of 45-50%. In addition, it is common that
your NQSO grant has less value and contains fewer shares versus
your earlier ISO grants.

Most well-established companies are not as generous with their option grants as the hot young start-ups. This leaves many people asking the question, "What am I still doing here? Where is the upside?" The tradeoff is the relative safety of an established company and the relative stability of the share price.

IF YOU ARE AN OLD PRO, REMEMBER

- Don't fall in love with your stock and options.
- Develop a clear financial plan.
- Consider diversification.
- Determine when to exercise.

FIVE

▼

LEAVING YOUR COMPANY

This is the one section of the book that will apply to every optionaire at some point. We strongly recommend that you read this chapter now and use it to plan for the day when you are no longer working for your current employer.

JOANNE LOSES THE FARM

Joanne left her company to start her own firm. She worked in an explosive industry, and was so overwhelmed that she did not focus on her options, as she should have. The day you leave your company the option expiration clock starts ticking. Most companies allow their employees between 30 and 90 days to exercise their vested options. If you miss the expiration date, you lose. Joanne knew that she was getting down to the wire and had to exercise the options any day, so she called her previous employer to get all the required paperwork to exercise her options. When she called, she was told that the options had expired two days before. The options had been worth $3.5 million (net of taxes). As you might imagine, she could not believe it. Joanne called her attorney; she called her CPA; she called her broker. She even considered calling Alan Greenspan. The answer was the same from all: "You're too late."

She lost the $3.5 million.

I am sure you are thinking to yourself that this could never happen to you. But Joanne was an intelligent person, just as you are. This kind of mistake happens more than you might imagine. You do not hear about it because it is not something people brag about.

A more common occurrence is that thousands of optionaires get a huge tax bill due to the exercise of their expiring options. Though it may be impossible to eliminate your tax liability, we are certain that forward planning can reduce the tax obligation that you may face.

JAMES JUST THOUGHT HE WAS RICH

At age 47, James Cole had thirteen years with his company. He felt he had had enough. He had enough of work, traffic, and office politics. He even had enough of his company's stock options. On a rainy February morning in Seattle, James gave six months notice, allowing the company plenty of time to find a replacement for his position. James' timing also ensured that all of his options would expire in that tax year, reducing the number of planning strategies that he could employ.

Later that week, he met with Human Resources and the stock plan administrator to review his benefits and employee options. James had 70,000 vested options: 56,000 ISOs granted at $3 and 14,000 NQSO granted at $8. The stock was trading at $78. James' gain was $4,200,000 on his ISOs and $980,000 on his NQSOs.

James remained bullish on the market, his company and the industry. All in all, he felt he was where he wanted to be financially. As you might have guessed, he missed a few key planning opportunities. Based upon his chosen lifestyle, he felt that he could retire with the gain from his options and his 401(k). However, what James failed to factor in were taxes—not just the income taxes due on the NQSOs, but more importantly, the AMT due on the ISOs he exercised and held the year he retired.

Due to the exercise and hold that James made on his ISOs, he owed 28% AMT on the gain of $4,200,000. The AMT due was approximately $1,200,000. Naturally, James did not have this kind of money lying around the house and had to sell stock and options to raise cash for taxes. This triggered an additional tax liability. In turn, he needed more money for taxes and the cycle repeated itself.

To fully understand James' story, additional background information is needed. James was always bullish on his company's stock performance so he made little effort to plan for the future. His ISOs had vested several years prior to his departure. When the ISOs first vested the stock was trading at $13 per share. If James had exercised and held his ISOs at that time he would have had a relatively small gain versus the $4,200,000 he faced when he left his company. Though he may not have completely avoided AMT at the time of exercise a few years ago, his current AMT liability would not be as substantial and all of his shares would have been held for over twelve months, qualifying for long-term capital gains.

DON'T LET JAMES' STORY BECOME YOUR STORY

There are several areas that James overlooked. Obviously, his greatest anguish was caused by failing to exercise the ISOs earlier. However, we want to clarify that we are not making a blanket statement that you must exercise your ISOs early, only that if James had, it would have helped him considerably. Any decision to exercise ISOs is individual, and should be made based on an application of the principles in this book to your unique circumstances, and with the help of qualified professionals.

THE PROS AND CONS OF EXERCISING AND HOLDING ISOs SOONER RATHER THAN LATER

Pros:
1.   Potential for less AMT. If the stock price appreciates, the amount of future AMT would be greater than if you exercised and held earlier.
2.   You will start the clock running to receive long-term capital gains on ISOs exercised and held. Under current tax law, shares need to be held for a minimum of twelve months from exercise and two years from grant date to qualify for long-term capital gains tax of 20%.

Cons:
1.   When you exercise and buy the shares, you have an out of pocket cash flow. Many optionaires do not have cash on hand early in their careers, and this makes exercising more difficult. Many of the larger brokerage firms will loan you the up front money in the form of a margin loan against your ISOs when you elect to exercise and hold.
2.   If the stock price falls after you exercise, you may have paid more in AMT than if you waited and exercised later on. Attempting to time the market, however, is a gamble.

WHEN TO EXERCISE?

The real questions are:

1.   Are you bullish on your company?
2.   Do you think your company's stock price will grow faster than the broader markets?

If you answered yes to both of these questions, serious

consideration should be given to exercising and holding your ISOs sooner rather than later. Generally, the opposite is recommended for NQSOs. In most cases, it is more advantageous to hold NQSOs until they are nearer their expiration date because they have no tax advantages to exercise early. Additionally, you may use a portion of your NQSOs after exercising and holding ISOs to minimize potential AMT. The higher your ordinary income, the greater your AMTI can be before AMT liability will affect you. Keep in mind, however, that waiting too long to exercise and sell your NQSOs forces you to exercise at the current market price. If the market plunges near your expiration date, you may have to exercise at a low price. If you are unsure of the related ramifications and potential tax liabilities, speak with your financial advisor prior to exercising. (See the *Investment Strategies* chapter for hedging ideas.)

WHAT YOU SHOULD CONSIDER IN YOUR PLANNING

1. **Start planning today**. There is little one can do to make up for lost time. Start your planning today, even if you do not intend to start exercising your options for a few more years.
2. **Determine your risk tolerance**. Quantifying your risk tolerance can be challenging to do on your own and is best accomplished by meeting with a financial advisor.
3. **It's volatility not taxes**. Most optionaires feel that taxes are their biggest nemesis. If you hold options in a company that experiences high market volatility, taxes may not be your worst enemy, since market volatility can cost you several times the potential tax savings. For stocks that historically experience annual price volatility of greater than 40%, you should base your plans first on market price movement, and second on tax implications.

4. **Don't be an ostrich**. It is always easier to stick your head in the sand, focus on your job and not look at what planning should be done today. This behavior must be avoided. Failing to create a realistic financial plan is worse than gambling. At least gamblers understand and play by the rules of the game.

THE STRATEGIC EXIT AND THE HASTY RETREAT

To the long-term planner who has been lining up an exit strategy for at least one year prior to leaving, we offer you congratulations on your vision. You will be able to reap the rewards due to your forethought. For everyone else here are a few areas to plan for:

Step 1 - Organize all your options.

Options should be organized by their vesting schedule, strike prices, option type. (See the Appendix for the *Employee Stock Option Worksheet*.)

Step 2 - Determine how bullish you are on the company.

Ask yourself the following questions:

- Do you feel your company will outperform the S&P 500? NASDAQ?
- Do you feel your company is one of the best investments available?
- What percent of your company stock do you want to hold on to for the long term?
- How did you come to this percentage?
- Is this an emotional decision or have you analyzed your situation?

Put your answers to the questions down on paper. Show them to a friend and bring them with you when you meet with your financial advisor. If you choose to hold a large percentage (50% or more of your portfolio in one company), then you could be demonstrating emotional investment behavior. In general, emotional investment decisions become bad investment decisions. When you show friends your answers, you may be surprised by the comments that you receive—especially if they do not work for your company. Their comments may sound something like "you're nuts," "what are you thinking?" or "I always considered you smart, but now. . . ." Please, realize that there are other quality companies and investment alternatives. Although diversification may lower your investment return, it should also reduce most portfolios' associated risk. This factor is critical in long-term planning. (Refer to the *Emotional Intelligence Quiz* in the Appendix.)

Step 3 - Should you use listed/OTC options against your vested option position?

Prior to trading options against your employee stock/options you MUST check with your company. Many companies prohibit some or all of their employees from trading options against their stock and employee options. If you are an officer, in addition to company restrictions, there may be SEC restrictions.

Benefits of listed and OTC options are, but not limited to:

1. Hedging downside price risk.
2. Creating current income without selling the underlying position.
3. Locking in your current gains.

For a further explanation of these planning ideas, see the Investment Strategies chapter.

Step 4 - How much money do you need (net worth and income)?

It's all about money, right? Obviously, the reason you are reading this book is to maximize your net worth and reduce your tax obligation. To ensure a "correct" exit strategy, be sure you can answer these basic questions:

- How much money and income do you need?
- How did you come to this conclusion?
- Required retirement income? Minimum desired? Gross or net income?
- How did you come to these figures?
- What is the required rate of return that your portfolio must produce for you to accomplish these goals?
- What strategies are you using to accomplish this?
- What have you done to protect your assets and ensure that your minimum required asset base is protected?

Many optionaires get a magic number in their head and shoot for this to be their net worth. Recently, $10,000,000 seems to be the most popular magic number. This reminds us of investors who feel that they must beat the S&P 500 performance. Why? What does the S&P 500 have to do with your personal financial goals? And why is $10,000,000 the goal so many people pick? Goals should be based on a careful evaluation of your future lifestyle needs, not because a particular number sounds good. Also, to ensure that your investment risk is in line with your goals, you must analyze your goals, quantify the required return and attempt to manage the associated risk. This can be a challenging process if you do not have a strong background in personal finance. Do not be shy about seeking professional help.

When an optionaire leaves his or her company, for whatever reasons, the change is often difficult. Not only is it challenging from a planning perspective, it is difficult on a personal level. Leaving behind a company that has made you wealthy can be a painful transition. But worse, most optionaires leave money on the table. The money is usually left in the form of options that have been granted, are in-the-money, but have not yet vested.

What can you do? Unfortunately, there is little you can do, except to remind yourself that there are more important issues in life. Be happy with the options you cashed in and the new-found wealth you have. Please do not let the money that remains torment you. It is almost impossible to get all the money off the table. If you do accomplish this, it usually means that new options have not been granted for several years, and if this was the case you might have been better off taking a risk and going to a company that would offer you more options and continue to provide them on an annual basis. Congratulations on the wealth you created. Your job now is to take care of your wealth and help it grow.

IF YOU ARE LEAVING YOUR COMPANY

- Start planning immediately.
- Decide when to exercise your ISOs (years in advance of your departure).
- Review the tax consequences of your actions.
- Develop strategies to get your money off the table.

SIX

▼

RESTRICTED AND CONTROL SECURITIES

What do Bill Gates, Michael Dell and Andy Grove have in common? Aside from having more money than everyone on your block combined, they are all insiders and hold restricted stock in the company they work for (and own). It is not just the big name CEOs and officers who have restrictions, but many everyday optionaires find themselves in a similar situation.

This section focuses on the issues that involve insiders and control persons. Due to the complexity of the legal and tax issues involved in this section, we have chosen to limit the information to general rules and regulations that insiders and control persons must be aware of. If you are an insider or think that you might be an insider, there is one simple rule to follow: Never sell stock or options without first consulting the legal counsel of the issuing firm. It is better to move slowly and miss a market opportunity than to rush ahead and violate Security Exchange Commission regulations.

RESTRICTED AND CONTROL SECURITIES

Restricted and control securities refer to securities that may be subject to special restrictions imposed by the Securities Exchange Commission (SEC). Common requirements for restricted and control securities are Rule 144, Rule 145 and the requirements for shelf-registered (S-3) sales.

CONTROL PERSON

Control persons, or insiders, are the directors, officers and substantial shareholders of corporations. In addition, this term can refer to charities, foundations, trusts, universities and other organizations. The SEC uses the term "affiliate" for a control person.

PRE-SALE CLEARANCE

It is essential that all control persons become familiar with the rules governing pre-sale clearance. Failure to accomplish this will lead to costly errors and the potential for legal problems.

For the sale to be "clean," the issuer's legal counsel must issue a legal option to the transfer agent prior to the sale stating that the specified security transaction is in compliance. Prior to issuing a legal option, counsel will require that they be provided with documentation from the seller's broker that all regulations and requirements have been complied with.

To summarize—at the time restricted securities are sold, the seller, the seller's broker, and the brokerage firm need to follow all presale restrictions. Working closely with the issuer's legal counsel and your brokerage firm's executive financial service group, you should be provided the necessary guidance. If you choose to use an independent or discount brokerage firm, you may find that they have limited or no access to the necessary resources and expertise.

RULE 144 REQUIREMENTS

There are four basic requirements that must be met to sell securities under Rule 144:

1. Adequate current information concerning the issuer must be publicly available.
2. A one-year holding period is required before Rule 144 "restricted securities" can be sold.
3. The amount of securities that can be sold in any three-month period for both listed and OTC companies is limited to the greater of one percent of the outstanding stock of the company or the average weekly trading

volume during the four calendar weeks preceding
receipt of the order to execute the transaction.

4. The seller must file a Form 144 in triplicate with the
   SEC and file a copy with the principal exchange
   where the security is traded, on the day of or prior to
   the day of sale.

LIMITATIONS ON AMOUNT OF SECURITIES SOLD

The limitation on sales within a three-month period is the
greater of:

1. 1% of outstanding shares based upon the most
   recently published reports by the issuer; or
2. average weekly trading volume that is reported
   during a four calendar weeks preceding a filing of
   form 144.

Here is an example. Blueshark.com has the following trading
volume over the past four weeks:

Wk 1	160,000
Wk 2	30,000
Wk 3	120,000
Wk 4	40,000

Blueshark.com has 10,000,000 outstanding shares. Under Rule
144, the seller could not sell more than 100,000 shares in a three-
month period. One percent of 10,000,000 shares is 100,000 shares,
and this amount is greater than the average volume of 87,500
shares (350,000/4).

All shares sold by the insider in question within the past three
months must be subtracted out of the above calculation. The
account activity of the person who has the restricted account
includes securities sold by relatives living in the same household,

entities in which the seller and relatives have a 10% interest or any trust where the seller or relative acts as trustee or executor.

SHORT SWING PROFITS—SECTION 16(C)

The Securities Exchange Act of 1934, Section 16(c), prohibits directors, corporate officers and 10% shareholders of the issuer from selling shares of said issuer short.

Owners of Rule 144 and 145 stock may enter into short transactions if the owner is not a director or officer, or a 10% shareholder of the issuer, and if applicable rules governing short sale rules are complied with when the short sale is placed.

When officers, directors, and 10% shareholders acquire or dispose of securities, a Form 4 must be filed with the SEC by the tenth day of the month following the month the transaction took place.

RED FLAGS AND DANGER SIGNS FOR INSIDERS

Prior to placing an order, you must review the following issues:

1. Did you buy the securities in the open market?
2. Are you an insider or affiliate, substantial shareholder, or a relative?
3. Was the stock a gift, pledge, or otherwise from an officer, director, substantial shareholder, or control person?
4. Is there a prospectus involved (shelf registration, S-3)?
5. Does the stock certificate have a legend on it? Just because there is no legend on the stock certificate does not mean there is no restriction.
6. Are you selling a large amount of stock relative to the number of outstanding shares?

At the risk of being redundant, we remind you once more that it is better to be cautious than to race ahead and cause problems for yourself and the issuer. There are few things more embarrassing for a corporate officer than to have their picture on the front page of the business section as the person fined and sanctioned by the SEC for inappropriate trading behavior involving their company stock.

SEVEN

▼

FREQUENTLY ASKED QUESTIONS

1. What is the difference between ISOs and NQSOs?

2. When should I exercise my employee stock options?

3. What does it cost to exercise employee stock options?

4. How soon can I exercise my employee stock options and when do they expire?

5. What do I need to do to exercise my employee stock options?

6. Are there issues to consider prior to selling stock?

7. Can I protect my paper gains without selling my stock or employee stock options?

8. What are the tax and economic benefits of ISOs?

9. What should I do prior to exercising ISOs?

10. What if the value of the stock declines after I exercise and hold my options?

11. Can I exercise and hold ISOs worth more than $100,000?

12. What are NQSOs?

13. What are the tax results of receiving a NQSO?

14. What is the tax result of exercising a NQSO?

15. Can capital losses offset NQSO gains?

16. How should I plan for my NQSOs at a company going public?

17. How can a taxpayer avoid postponing the compensation income until restrictions lapse for stock purchased using NQSOs?

18. What is Alternative Minimum Tax (AMT) and how does it relate to planning for exercising ISOs?

19. How do I recover AMT?

20. Can I get a credit against my ordinary tax for the AMT?

21. Can I offset AMT with deductions?

22. How is AMT calculated for a private company?

23. What tax rates apply for long-term capital gains?

24. What are the tax results if the option is sold before it is exercised?

25. Early exercise provisions: 83(b) election, does it make sense?

26. What is the advantage of making the Section 83(b) election?

27. What are the disadvantages of making the Section 83(b) election?

28. What is the value of my options at a private company?

29. What if the employer is acquired, resulting in a buy-out of the options or an exchange for new options?

30. If I want to quit or retire, how long do I have to exercise?

31. What should insiders know?

32. How can I raise cash to exercise and hold my employee stock options?

33. Do I have to hold the shares that I exercised at the brokerage firm that administers my company's option plan?

34. Can I use listed options against non-vested options?

35. What rules apply when the stock received is not freely transferable or is subject to a risk of forfeiture?

36. Should I make gifts of non-qualified options for estate planning? What is the tax impact of doing this?

1.   What is the difference between ISOs and NQSOs?

There are two types of options that you may receive in your employee compensation package: Incentive Stock Options (ISOs) and Non-Qualified Stock Options (NQSOs). The fundamental difference between the two is in their tax treatment. ISOs may receive preferential tax treatment, whereas NQSOs are taxed as ordinary income at the time of exercise.

HOW STOCKS / OPTIONS ARE TAXED		
	Regular Tax	Alternative Min. Tax
N Q S O s		
• Date of Grant	N/A	N/A
• Date of Exercise	Spread is Taxable (1)	Same as Regular Tax
• Date of Sale	Taxable (2)	Same as Regular Tax
I S O s		
• Date of Grant	N/A	N/A
• Date of Exercise	N/A	Spread is Taxable (3)
• Date of Sale	Taxable (4)	Taxable (5)
E S P P		
• Date of Grant	N/A	N/A
• Date of Exercise	N/A	Spread is Taxable
• Date of Sale	Taxable (6)	Taxable

Notes:

(1) Spread equals fair market value at the date of exercise less option price; will be subject to withholding at 28% federal and state tax; tax basis is now cost plus taxable spread.

(2) Gain is equal to sales price less tax basis; long-term capital gain is applicable to stock held more than 12 months (effective January 1, 1998).

(3) Spread generally not subject to income tax withholding; tax basis equals option price plus alternative minimum taxable spread.

(4) Taxable gain equals sales price less option price.

(5) Taxable gain equals sales price less option price less spread taxed at exercise.

(6) The definition of a qualifying and disqualifying disposition for ESPP is generally the same as ISOs.

2. When should I exercise my employee options?

When to exercise employee stock options is likely the most frequently asked question among all optionaires. However, because each individual's situation is different, there is no definitive answer. The following are generalizations:

We typically recommend exercising ISOs and holding the underlying stock sooner rather than later, taking advantage of the 83(b) election, if available, and exercising and selling NQSOs closer to their expiration.

To determine when it is appropriate for you to exercise your options, the real questions are:

1. Are you bullish on your company?
2. Do you think your company's stock price will grow faster than the broader markets?

If you answered yes to both of these questions, give serious consideration to exercising and holding your ISOs sooner rather than later. If you are unsure of the related ramifications and potential tax liabilities, speak with your financial advisor prior to exercising your options.

What you should consider in your exercise planning:

1. **Start planning today.** There is little one can do to make up for lost time. Start your planning today, even if you do not intend to start exercising your options for a few more years.
2. **It's volatility, not taxes.** Most optionaires feel that taxes are their biggest nemesis. If you hold options in a company that experiences high market volatility,

taxes may not be your worst enemy since market volatility can cost you several times the potential tax savings. A stock that historically experiences market volatility of over 40% should be planned around the market price movement first, and taxes second.

3. **Don't be an ostrich.** It is always easier to stick your head in the sand, focus on your job, and not look at what planning should be done today. This behavior must be avoided. To avoid creating a realistic financial plan is worse than gambling. At least most gamblers understand and play by the rules of the game.

For further explanation on these recommendations, refer to the following questions:

1. What are the tax and economic benefits of Incentive Stock Options? (#8)
2. What are the advantages and disadvantages of the Section 83(b) election? (#s 26, 27)
3. What is the tax result of exercising a non-qualified option? (#14)

3. What does it cost to exercise employee stock options?

To exercise ISOs or NQSOs, you will have to pay an amount equal to the exercise price of the employee stock options being exercised times the number of shares you are exercising.

For example: Beth Smith has a grant of 10,000 ISOs with an exercise price of $5 per share. To exercise these options, she will have to pay $50,000 (10,000 ISOs x $5 exercise price = $50,000).

When exercising options, you may incur administrative costs charged by the brokerage firm administering your option plan. In addition, when you exercise and sell or hold your NQSOs, taxes will be withheld at the time of the exercise.

4. How soon can I exercise my employee stock options and when do they expire?

Generally, most options expire between five and ten years from grant date. Please note that every company has its own vesting and expiration plan. Your stock plan administrator can give you the full details.

For example: Sue was granted a total of 57,000 options over a five-year period. Her first option grant vested on 01/01/95 and expires on 12/31/05. Sue can exercise each grant of options at any time in between their vesting date and expiration date. Restrictions may apply.

SUE'S OPTIONS						
Option Grant	Date of Grant	Option Type	Number of Shares	Vesting Date	Expiration Date	Exercise Price
0001	1/1/90	ISO	10,000	1/1/95	12/31/05	$5.00
0002	1/1/91	ISO	10,000	1/1/96	12/31/06	$7.00
0003	1/1/92	NQSO	12,000	1/1/97	12/31/07	$10.00
0004	1/1/93	NQSO	15,000	1/1/98	12/31/08	$14.50
0005	1/1/94	NQSO	10,000	1/1/99	12/31/09	$22.00

For Grant 0001, Sue can exercise the options between 1/1/95 and 12/31/05. For Grant 0002, Sue can exercise the options between 1/1/96 and 12/31/06, and so on.

5. What do I need to do to exercise my employee stock options?

Because every company has different policies and procedures regarding employee stock and options, you will need to consult your stock plan administrator for the specific terms of your position. Outlined below are the *general* rules and guidelines that you will need to complete to exercise your employee stock options.

   1.   Open an account with the approved administrating

brokerage firm(s) that is exercising your options. This firm(s) has been pre-selected by your company.

2. Get an updated option grant summary from your stock plan administrator. This information should contain the following:
    • date of grant
    • option type (ISO, NQSO)
    • number of shares
    • vesting date
    • expiration date
    • exercise price
    (See *Employee Stock Option Worksheet* in the Appendix.)

3. Review your options with your financial advisor for potential tax and market volatility issues.

4. Check that your vested options are on file with your approved administrating brokerage firm(s) and that your options are ready to be exercised. For options to be exercisable, they must be vested and approved by the company stock plan administrator. In addition, required forms generally must be forwarded to the brokerage firm you are using.

5. If you plan on exercising and holding your options (buying), transfer money to the approved broker prior to the exercise. Some companies allow their employees to exercise and hold options internally by sending a check directly to the stock plan administrator.

6. When you place an order of any kind, make sure that you do not have any outstanding orders on the books.

For example: you placed a Limit Order on your stock a few months ago at $80 for 1,000 shares when the stock was trading at $60. The share price never reached $80; thus the order was not executed. Today you wish to sell the same 1,000 shares at the current market price (less than $80), and place a market order. You must cancel the existing order; the brokerage firm does not do it for you. If you fail to cancel the order, when the share price goes to $80, the old order will be executed, even though you may no longer hold those shares or even be an employee of the company. The net effect of this is that you would be short 1,000 shares and for every dollar the stock prices goes up you lose $1,000 (1,000 shares x $1).

6. Are there issues to consider prior to selling stock?

The tax considerations are only one factor in making a decision to sell stock received by the exercise of ISOs. Tax results of different scenarios should be estimated. What is the benefit from the maximum capital gains rate? What is the interrelation of gains to be reported, alternative minimum tax credits that are carried forward, tax preference adjustments from exercising ISOs, and deductions that are disallowed for the AMT, such as state income taxes?

There are also tax accounting issues involved. Tracking multiple blocks of stock in a brokerage account can be very complex. The general rule for tax reporting purposes is shares that can't be identified are accounted for on a first-in, first-out basis. A taxpayer can overcome this rule by giving the broker written instructions to sell specific blocks of stock, "such as sell the 500 shares of Megatech Stock I acquired on April 15, 1997." Identifying shares sold as those with the highest tax basis can result in a substantial reduction of the current income tax.

Employers rely on their employees for notification about sales and transfers that result in compensation to be reported on the employee's W-2 and deducted on the employer's income tax return. The employer will need to know the date the option was exercised, the date of sale, the option price and the fair market value on the date of exercise, and if the value of the stock has declined after the date of exercise, the sale price of the stock. If the employee sells shares shortly after exercising an ISO, while holding shares previously acquired, the compensation amount could be reported in error. The employee must be careful or multiple tax adjustments could result (in short, a mess!).

The economic considerations are more important than the tax considerations when making decisions about selling stock. Having almost all of an investment portfolio in one stock exposes the employee to unnecessary and unwise market risk. Once one has built wealth, it's wise to protect it through diversification. As the old saying goes, "Pigs get fat, hogs get slaughtered!" The dramatic reductions in rates applying to long-term capital gains for stock held more than 12 months will result in more reticence in adopting early diversification strategies.

Cash flow requirements may also dictate the sale of stock, including the requirement to pay taxes (including alternative minimum taxes.) Timing the sale according to when the tax payments are required can result in deferring or postponing the tax, enabling the employee to squeeze out additional investment income.

7. **Can I protect my paper gains without selling my stock or employee options?**
Of course you can. You do not have to sell your stock or employee stock options to lock in gains or protect yourself from downside loss. Popular strategies that we commonly recommend include, but are not limited to: collars, hedge puts, in-the-money calls, margin, and exchange funds. (Refer to the *Investment Strategies* chapter for further explanation.)

8. **What are the tax and economic benefits of ISOs?**
An employee may control shares of corporate stock for a limited time for no investment. Therefore, the employee may enjoy potential capital appreciation with no risk.

When the stock has appreciated and the employee exercises the option to purchase the stock, no taxable income is currently recognized for the excess of the fair market value of the stock over the purchase price (or "spread"). The "spread" is considered a tax preference in computing the alternative minimum tax.

The "spread" at exercise will be taxed as a long-term capital gain when the stock is sold, provided that the holding period rules are met. In order to qualify for long-term capital gains treatment, the stock must be held more than two years from the date of grant and one year from the date of exercise. The tax rates that apply to the gain are discussed below. The date of grant is the date on which the board of directors or the stock option committee completes the corporate action constituting an offer of stock pursuant to the terms of the option, rather than the date on which the option agreement is prepared. The date of exercise is the date on which the grantor corporation receives notice of exercise of the option and payment for the stock, rather than the date the shares of stock are actually transferred.

If the holding period is not met, the lesser of the "spread" at exercise or the gain from the sale of the stock is taxable as ordinary compensation income. The gain on sale limitation is not available for a transaction where a loss would not be recognized, such as a wash sale, a transfer to a charitable remainder trust, or a sale to a related party.

(Under the wash sale rules, a current deduction is disallowed for a loss from the sale of stock or securities when, within a period beginning 30 days before the date of sale and ending 30 days after that date, the taxpayer has acquired or entered into a contract or option to acquire, substantially identical stock or securities.)

Since the maximum federal income tax rate that applies to long-term capital gains is generally 20%, meeting the holding period requirements is important for all employees who are planning with respect to incentive stock options.

If ordinary income results to the employee from not meeting the holding period requirements, the employer will receive a tax deduction for the "compensation" element with no cash outlay required.

9. What should I do prior to exercising ISOs?

There are a number of considerations in planning to exercise ISOs.

If you have some latitude in timing when the ISOs may be exercised, then a computation may be made to compare the AMT with the regular tax to minimize the AMT liability.

Stock that is identical to the stock to be received may be exchanged at face value to pay the exercise price in exercising ISOs as a tax-free exchange. The old shares are surrendered in payment for the new shares, and no taxable gain or loss is reported for the transaction. This is called "pyramiding." However, stock acquired by exercise of an ISO that has not yet been held for the required period will not qualify for this type of exchange.

For example, Jane employee has 100 shares of Supergrow stock with a total fair market value of $5,000 ($50 per share), for which she paid $50, or $.50 per share. She has an incentive stock option to purchase 5,000 shares of Supergrow stock for $1 per share. If Supergrow permits it, Jane may surrender her 100 shares and receive 5,000 shares in return. Her tax basis in the shares received will be $.50 per share for 100 shares, the basis of the 100 shares surrendered, and zero for the remaining 4,900 received shares. She will have no taxable gain or loss for the exchange. She will still report a tax preference of $250,000 (value of shares received) - $5,000 (option price) = $245,000 in computing the alternative minimum tax for the year of exercise.

10. What if the value of the stock declines after I exercise and hold my options?

One of worst scenarios for an employee who exercises an ISO is for the value of the stock to fall dramatically in a later year. The reason is the employee must pay taxes on non-cash income. The employee may have to raise the cash from other sources to pay the tax.

To illustrate the effect of a market decline for an employee, we have created some federal tax projections under several scenarios. The taxpayer is a single person with wages of $100,000, who only claims one personal exemption and the standard deduction.

In 1998, the taxpayer exercises a stock option with the difference between the option price of the stock and the fair market value of the stock is $200,000. In 1999, the taxpayer sells the stock for its option price. (In other words, the market has erased the appreciation that existed in 1998.)

- If the taxpayer only reported wages income of $100,000 for 1998 and 1999, the total federal income tax would be about $47,400.
- If the taxpayer exercised an incentive stock option, the total federal income tax for 1998 and 1999 would be about $80,500. The taxpayer would have $33,000 of minimum tax credits available to reduce regular tax liabilities in a later year. $23,700 of the credits would have been used in 1999.
- If the taxpayer exercised a non-qualified stock option, the total federal income tax liability for 1998 and 1999 would be about $118,328. The taxpayer would have a $197,000 unused capital loss carryover to be applied in a later year. Clearly, this taxpayer had little to lose by selling at least some of the stock when the option was exercised.

What would happen if the taxpayer sold some additional stock for a $200,000 long-term capital gain in 1999?

- If the taxpayer only reported wages income, the taxpayer would have a total income tax liability for 1998 and 1999 of about $89,700.
- If the taxpayer exercised an incentive stock option, the taxpayer would have a total income tax liability for 1998 and 1999 of $93,750. The taxpayer would have about $5,500 of minimum tax credits to be used in a later year.

- If the taxpayer exercised a non-qualified stock option, the taxpayer would have a total income tax liability for 1998 and 1999 of $97,725. The $200,000 capital gain would absorb all of the capital losses from the option shares.

What lessons can we learn from these scenarios?
- Market risk should be a concern when tax planning for employee stock options.
- Employees who exercise non-qualified stock options should seriously consider selling at least enough of the shares they receive to pay the income taxes they owe.
- If the value of the shares has declined when they are sold, the employee should seek other sources of income, particularly capital gains, to use capital losses for shares purchased using non-qualified options and minimum tax credits for shares purchased using incentive stock options.

11. Can I exercise and hold ISOs worth more than $100,000?
(The following is an email we received from a client and our response.)

Is $100,000 the annual limit that can be exercised in a year, or the maximum that can be exercised in a year, or both? For example, if I was granted $100,000 worth in each of three consecutive years, could I exercise all $300,000 in one year, hold for a year, and only pay long-term capital gains?

The rule is the maximum fair market value of stock that is exercisable for the first time by any individual during a calendar year is $100,000. The fair market value of the shares is determined on the date of grant. Any options in excess of this amount that are exercisable during the calendar year are treated as non-qualified stock options. The earliest-granted options will be treated as incentive stock options. (Internal Revenue Code Section 422[d])

The email question is based upon when the options were granted. It's not possible to predict the result. However, if $100,000 worth of options becomes exercisable in three consecutive years ($100,000 per year), you could exercise $300,000 worth in year three and eventually qualify for long-term capital gains treatment for the regular tax.

12. What are Non-Qualified Stock Options (NQSOs)?

The reason these options are called "non-qualified" is that they do not qualify for special treatment as does another type of option, called incentive stock options (ISOs).

A NQSO is a way for a company to compensate employees or service providers without paying cash. Instead, the company grants the employee or service provider an option to purchase shares of stock at a fixed price. The price is about the amount the stock is trading for when the stock is publicly traded. When the stock isn't publicly traded, the company determines the value of a share of stock on the date the option is granted. The option typically lapses on a certain date. The incentive to the employee or service provider is to participate in the potential increase in value of the stock without having to risk a cash investment.

Since this arrangement is a form of compensation, the employee or service provider generally must report ordinary income when the option is exercised. The amount of ordinary income is the excess of the fair market value of the shares received over the option price. The company receives a tax deduction for this ordinary income element reported by the employee or service provider.

Incentive stock options are only available for employees and other restrictions apply for them. For regular tax purposes, ISOs have the advantage that no income is reported when the option is exercised and, if certain requirements are met, the entire gain when the stock is sold is taxed as long-term capital gains.

13. What are the tax results of receiving NQSOs?

No taxable income usually results when an employee or service provider receives a non-qualified stock option. Since the options typically aren't actively traded on an established market, they are deemed to not have an ascertainable fair market value at the time of grant.

14. What is the tax result of exercising NQSOs?

The excess of the fair market value on the exercise date of the stock received over the option price is generally taxable as ordinary compensation income. The stock receives a tax basis (cost to determine capital gain or loss) of the fair market value on the date of exercise, and the holding period for the stock commences with the date of exercise. If the recipient is an employee, the employer should report the income on Form W-2. If the recipient is not an employee, the company should report the income on Form 1099-Miscellaneous.

Special rules apply when the stock received is subject to restrictions that prevent the recipient from selling it.

15. Can capital losses offset NQSO gains?

(The following is an email we received from a client and our response.)

> Can an individual offset gain from a same-day NQSO exercise with short-term capital loss? Since this gain shows up in my W-2, may I somehow list it on my schedule D?

Since the gain from a same-day sale of stock acquired with a non-qualified employee stock option is ordinary income, it is properly reported by an employee as wages, not capital gains. Only up to $3,000 of net capital losses may be deducted from other income, including the income from non-qualified options.

Since you sold the stock, at least you should have the cash to pay the tax. Your employer should have withheld some taxes from your sale proceeds.

16. How should I plan for my NQSOs at a company going public?

(The following is an email we received from a client and our response.)

> Right now I have NQSOs in a private company which plans to go public within 2 years. If I exercise these options, I understand the spread between the option price and the "Fair Market Value" will be taxed as ordinary income. My question is: how is the "Fair Market Value" determined for a company which is not public yet? Can the company arbitrarily set a price we have to live with?

When a company is not public yet, an employee has little choice but to rely on the figures given to him or her by the company as the fair market value. To have an appraisal done to determine yourself if it is prohibitively expensive would cost $15,000 to $20,000, and requires extensive time and cooperation by the company's accounting personnel and accounting firm.

17. How can a taxpayer avoid postponing the compensation income until restrictions lapse for stock purchased using NQSOs?

The taxpayer may elect under Internal Revenue Code Section 83(b) to report the ordinary income amount as of the date of exercise of the option. *The election is required even when the income amount is zero and must be made within 30 days after exercising the option!*

The election is made by filing a written statement with the Internal Revenue Service office where the taxpayer files his or her income tax return. A copy of the election statement is also attached to the income tax return for the date of exercise, and another copy is given to the employer.

The election may only be revoked with the consent of the Commissioner of the IRS.

18. What is Alternative Minimum Tax and how does it relate to planning for exercising incentive stock options?

The alternative minimum tax (AMT) was created so that taxpayers with substantial income would pay some tax. Many voters were outraged by statistics published by the Treasury Department showing that many taxpayers had substantial income, but were able to avoid paying income taxes using tax deductions, incentive tax credits and tax sheltered investments.

The Federal income tax is actually a parallel tax system. There is a "regular" tax that most of us are fairly familiar with. There is also an "alternative minimum tax" (AMT). The tax is computed using both methods, and you generally pay the higher tax. If the alternative minimum tax does apply, a portion of the excess over the regular tax may be available as a tax credit in a later year, treated somewhat like a prepayment of the later year's tax.

The alternative minimum tax rates are 26% for the first $175,000 of alternative minimum taxable income (AMTI) and 28% for AMTI over $175,000. The maximum rates as described above for the regular tax for sales of capital assets on or after January 1, 1998, will also apply for the alternative minimum tax. Single persons have an AMT exemption of $33,750, phased out by 25% of the excess of AMTI over $112,500, and eliminated for AMTI of $247,500 or more. The AMT exemption on a joint return for married persons is $45,000, phased out by 25% of the excess of AMTI over $150,000, and eliminated for AMTI of $330,000 or more.

Major deductions disallowed in computing the alternative minimum tax include itemized deductions for property taxes, state personal income taxes and certain miscellaneous itemized deductions. Interest expense from home equity lines of credit may also be disallowed.

Many taxpayers who prepare their own income tax returns and some tax return preparers have ignored the AMT because they aren't aware of it, don't understand it, or believe it doesn't apply. However, we are finding the tax applies more and more often, including for middle class taxpayers. It has been estimated that the

AMT applied to about 600,000 taxpayers in 1995 and will apply to six million taxpayers in 2006.

The AMT is important to consider when preparing income tax returns and in tax planning computations. When the tax situation is planned in advance, you can avoid wasting deductions disallowed under the AMT. You can also prepare in advance for the cash required to pay the tax, be sure estimated tax payment requirements are met, and plan to use minimum tax credits.

The alternative minimum tax is a critical concern with regard to ISOs. The excess of the fair market value on the date of exercise over the option price is considered a "tax preference" that is added to regular taxable income in computing the alternative minimum taxable income (AMTI) for the year of exercise. Note the new rates for long-term capital gains do not apply to this "spread" amount in the year of exercise. Since major deductions are disallowed for AMT and the maximum AMT tax rate is 28% (even considering the reduced rates applying for long-term capital gains), it is quite common for the AMT to apply in the year of exercise of an ISO.

19. How do I recover AMT?

The alternative minimum tax that results from timing differences, such as the ISO adjustment, is carried over and may be used as a tax credit in a later year when the regular tax exceeds the AMT. No tax credit is allowed for the AMT that results from disallowed deductions, such as property taxes, state income taxes and miscellaneous itemized deductions. The general rule is the AMT credit may be applied up to the excess of the regular tax liability over the tentative minimum tax liability.

For ISOs, the credit typically is not all recovered in the year the stock is sold because the regular tax rate for long-term capital gains is 20%, while the AMT rate for the tax preference is 26% or 28%. Thus, there is about 6% or 8% of unused credit to be used against other taxable income.

Does this additional credit have much value? As usual, the answer is "That depends . . . . " The result is if the AMT credit isn't used on the previous year's tax return, it will be reduced on the current year's tax return.

Apparently, Congress is determined that taxpayers should not receive a tax benefit for their state income taxes and other exclusion items when determining the availability of the AMT credit carryover.

You should plan on paying the 26% or 28% federal tax with respect to the tax preference for ISOs. Any benefit that you receive for the AMT credit is icing on the cake.

However, don't let the "tax tail wag the dog" when planning these transactions. The objective is to maximize what you keep. Don't walk away from a substantial gain just because it results in a tax.

AMT considerations can force an employee to sell shares of stock to generate the cash needed to pay income taxes. Alternatively, the employee could borrow the amount needed to pay the tax using a margin loan secured by the stock. (The interest is not deductible for a loan when the proceeds are used to pay personal income taxes.)

20. Can I get a credit against my ordinary tax for the AMT?

(The following is an email we received from a client and our response.)

> I will be required to pay AMT because I exercised some ISOs. I am trying to figure out if selling the stock this year and thus paying short-term capital gains on the stock at 36% but eliminating AMT is better than waiting 12 months for the long-term gain of 20% on the stock and paying the AMT.

Not if you want to pay the lowest tax. If you exercise the option in this year, incurring an AMT, and sell the shares next year after the required holding period, you will be able to apply some of your AMT credit to reduce your tax next year. Since the federal

AMT rate (in most cases) is 28% and the regular rate for long-term capital gains is 20%, you will only be able to apply about two-thirds of your AMT credit. The excess is carried over and may be reduced for various reasons.

Also, bear in mind that if the price of the stock goes down, you may not get as much benefit for the AMT credit. You could end up with an AMT capital loss, limited to $3,000.

21. Can I offset AMT with deductions?

(The following is an email we received from a client and our response.)

I know I will be subjected to AMT next year. I was wondering if there is anything I can do to create more deductions for AMT so that I minimize the AMT bill. For example, I understand that the mortgage interest payments on a primary house is deductible under AMT. So I bought a house (I was going to buy a house sooner or later anyway, but this I think will help reduce my AMT bill). I want to know if there are any such deductions that I could create?

A home acquisition mortgage is one of a very few deductions that are allowed for the alternative minimum tax. Charitable contributions are another one, if you are so inclined.

Medical deductions are usually eliminated because they are subject to a 10% of adjusted gross income floor.

Investment interest (interest incurred to buy investments that generate taxable investment income) is deductible for AMT up to the amount of your investment income.

If you have a business that generates a loss, that loss may be deductible for AMT. There are many tax sections that could eliminate the deduction, so you would do well to consult with a tax advisor on this one.

You should be aware that deductions for state income taxes and real estate taxes are not allowed for the AMT.

22. How is AMT calculated for a private company?

(The following is an email we received from a client and our response.)

> I've exercised ISOs this year, but because our company was not public at the time, I don't know what number to use for the AMT calculation. The IRS regulations specify that the tax liability is the difference between the option price and the market price of the stock on the day of exercise. If there is no market for the stock, how should the difference be calculated?

You should go to the individual responsible for employee benefits or administration of your company's ISO plan and ask for the fair market value of the stock at the date of exercise. It's impractical for you to determine a value, but the stock still has a value, even when it's not publicly traded. Since the company has provided you with this benefit, the company should provide the information you need to prepare your income tax returns.

23. What tax rates apply for long-term capital gains?

The maximum 20% long-term capital gains rate applies to most sales of securities held more than one year.

For assets sold after December 31, 2000, another long-term rate of 18% will apply for assets held more than five years. In addition, individuals in the 15% tax bracket may qualify for a 10% tax rate for long-term capital gains, 8% for assets sold after December 31, 2000, held more than five years.

Special election. For capital assets sold after December 31, 2000, capital assets held more than five years will qualify for the 18%/8% rate. For individuals in a tax bracket higher than 15%, the five-year rate will only apply to capital assets acquired after December 31, 2000. A special election will be available to treat assets as acquired on January 1, 2001. For individuals in the 15% tax bracket, assets acquired before January 1, 2001, will also qualify for five-year treatment. The election may be used for tradable stock, other capital assets, and property used in a trade or business.

Effect of election. If a taxpayer elects to have an asset treated as acquired on January 1, 2001, the asset will be treated as sold on that date. Tax must be paid on any gain from the deemed sale, but losses will not be recognized.

24. What are the tax results if the option is sold before it is exercised?

If the option is sold or otherwise disposed of in an arm's length transaction, the money plus the fair market value of any property received is taxable as ordinary compensation income.

In addition, if the transaction is not arm's length, such as to certain related persons, when the person who buys the option exercises it, the service provider will also recognize ordinary compensation income for the fair market value of the stock received over the amount paid. The person who bought the stock receives a basis adjustment for the income reported by the service provider in the year of exercise.

For example, Jane sells an option she received from her employer, XYZ Corp., to her daughter, Joanne, for $1,000 in 1997. During 1998, Jane exercises the option. The option price is $4,000. The fair market value on the exercise date of the stock received is $10,000. Joanne sells the stock during 1999 for $20,000.

Jane has taxable ordinary compensation income for 1997 of $1,000, the amount received from Joanne.

Jane has taxable ordinary compensation income for 1998 of $5,000—the $10,000 fair market value of the stock received less Joanne's $1,000 investment in the option and the $4,000 option price.

Joanne has a capital gain in 1999 of $10,000—$20,000 sale price less her original $1,000 investment in the option, the $4,000 option price and the $5,000 ordinary income reported by Jane in 1998.

(The holding period for the stock begins on the date of exercise of the option.)

25. Early exercise provisions: 83(b) election, does it make sense?

Some employers permit employees to exercise their incentive stock options before they are vested. The stock received is subject to repurchase by the company at the option price if the employee leaves before the vesting requirements are met.

This can help employees to meet the holding period requirements sooner and can reduce the tax preference from exercise. In order to secure these benefits, the taxpayer must file an election under Section 83(b) of the Internal Revenue Code.

The general rule when an employee receives restricted property (unvested stock) relating to his or her employment is the property received is valued when the restrictions lapse. When an employee makes a Section 83(b) election, he or she is electing to have the restrictions disregarded and the property valued on the date received.

The election must be made within 30 days of exercising the option (certified mail recommended). It is sent to the Internal Revenue Service, a copy is given to the employer, and a copy is attached to the income tax return for the year of election.

For example, Peach Company permits employees to exercise their ISOs early. Peach is planning an initial public offering of its stock in six months, so the employees exercise their options early. The option price is $1. The estimated fair market value at exercise is $2. When the stock is vested after the IPO, the stock is trading at $100. If an employee makes a Section 83(b) election, his or her preference will be $1 per share. If an employee does not make the election, his or her preference will be $99 per share.

26. What is the advantage of making the Section 83(b) election?

If the stock rises in value after the exercise of the option, the gain after the exercise date is taxable as a capital gain, potentially eligible for a 20% tax rate for a long-term capital gain. The maximum federal income tax rate for ordinary income is 39.6%.

27. What are the disadvantages of making the Section 83(b) election?

If the stock declines in value after the exercise of the option, the loss after the exercise date is a capital loss. Capital losses are only deductible to the extent of capital gains plus $3,000 per year. Excess capital losses may be carried over to subsequent years.

If the stock appreciates, the corporation loses the tax deduction for the increase in value after the date of exercise.

28. What is the value of my options at a private company?

(The following is an email we received from a client and our response.)

I am working for a company preparing to go public in the next 12-18 months. They have given me some stock options.

1. How do I calculate the value of the options when the company goes public? For instance, if there are 100 million shares and I have 10,000 options, is there a formula that relates to their relative value?
2. For argument's sake, let's say the company is valued at 250 million when it goes public. How do you calculate value per share?
3. Is there a relationship between the number of shares/options one has relative to the total number of shares?

Your three questions essentially boil down to one—how do I value my employer's stock for these transactions when it's not publicly traded?

The short answer is, you shouldn't have to. Go to whoever is responsible for employee benefits in your company and request that the company provide a letter with the information you need, which is the fair market value of the stock on the date of exercise or when restrictions lapse.

Valuation is a very complex issue and determining it is an expensive proposition. Since the employer is providing these options to you, the employer should also provide the information you need for tax planning and for preparing your income tax returns.

For non-qualified options, the employer may be required to report the spread between the fair market value of the stock and the option price as additional compensation with your payroll information, and to withhold payroll taxes.

29. What if the employer is acquired, resulting in a buy-out of the options or an exchange for new options?

If an acquiring party purchases the outstanding NQSOs from employees or service providers, the money plus the fair market value of any property received by the employees or service providers is taxable as ordinary compensation income.

The IRS has ruled that no taxable income resulted when a company was reorganized in a tax-free reorganization and non-qualified stock options for the new company were issued in exchange for outstanding stock options of the old company.

30. If I want to quit or retire, how long do I have to exercise?

The day you leave your company, the option expiration clock starts ticking. Most companies allow their employees between 30 and 90 days to exercise their vested options. If the expiration day goes by you lose. (See *Leaving Your Company* chapter for more detail.)

31. What should insiders know?

Corporate insider issues are beyond the scope of this presentation.

Relatively recent changes in the securities laws have removed most of the restrictions on key executives for stock received by exercise of an incentive stock option.

The IRS has not updated an older ruling that indicates the

restrictions under securities law Section 16(b) are a substantial risk of forfeiture. It may be an "insider" should file an election under Internal Revenue Code Section 83(b) (explained above) to fix the date to determine the "spread" adjustment for the exercise of the ISO. Otherwise, the date could be postponed by six months. Remember that the election should be made within 30 days after exercising the option. (See *Restricted and Controlled Securities* chapter for more detail.)

32. How can I raise cash to exercise and hold my employee stock options?

If you are bullish on your company, do not mind holding a concentrated position, and are willing to take some risk, a few ways to raise cash to exercise and hold your options are:

1. **Margin**: The use of margin is a strategy that involves using stock as collateral for a loan. The shareholder may typically borrow up to 50% of the value of their freely tradable, margin-eligible equity positions. The amount of credit extended to the shareholder will vary depending upon the purpose of the loan, the number of shares outstanding, the stock's daily trading volume and other factors set by the Federal Reserve and the shareholder's chosen brokerage firm. (Refer to the *Investment Strategies* chapter for further explanation.)

2. **Sell to cover**: When using a sell to cover strategy, you will sell a portion of your options to pay for the cost of exercising and holding the remaining shares. The effectiveness of the strategy varies because you effectively reduce your underlying stock position in half due to the tax obligation on the exercise. There is no present formula to determine the viability of this strategy; please review with your advisor.

3. **Out of pocket**: Use funds from outside sources to buy and hold options. In general, this is not a recommended strategy. If you have a large position in your company stock or still have options outstanding, you are increasing the risk profile of your portfolio by adding additional shares of your company stock into the portfolio.

4. **Covered calls**: Call options are securities that give the holder the right to buy the underlying stock at a specific price by a certain date. To raise cash for an exercise, you can write calls against existing shares for a premium. (Refer to the *Investment Strategies* chapter for further explanation.)

33. Do I have to hold the shares that I exercised at the brokerage firm that administers my company's option plan?

No. Once you exercise your options and have shares long in your account, you can transfer the shares to another brokerage firm.

34. Can I use listed options against non-vested options?

Yes. Options that have been granted to you but have not yet vested are paper money. Until you vest and exercise your options, you are only a paper optionaire. Here are a few strategies you can employ to lock in paper gains even though you have not yet vested:

1. You can use a hedge put on your company stock or sector index for NQSOs and ISOs.
2. If you choose to collar unvested options, there are several important points that you need to be aware of and that you should review with your financial advisor. Also, this strategy should only be considered for ISOs unless you hold the equivalent number of shares long in your brokerage account.
   - Collars written against positions that you do not

hold, and/or that are not long in your account are considered to be uncovered or "naked." This means that that you do not have the shares to cover the transaction if you are called away. When one writes a collar against non-vested options, what they are doing is buying a put to protect against downside price movement. On the other side of the transaction, you are selling a call option, which allows the buyer to purchase your shares at a stated price by a specific date. To summarize, if the holder of the call option chooses to buy/call your shares, you will be forced to sell your options.

- The potential for problems comes if you are called prior to your options vesting. In that case, what shares would you send to the holder of your call? To meet this obligation you would need to have other shares to transfer to the holder of the call or enough cash to settle the transaction. Being called early can cause problems for you if you are not prepared. Fortunately, there are ways to deal with this. One solution is to have other shares of the same stock long in a brokerage account that can cover the call.

The two major risks of this strategy are:

1. You leave your employer prior to vesting the options and you lose the options you purchased. The cost in dollar terms would be the number of options you exercised multiplied by the strike price you paid.
2. The stock price falls below your exercise price and you did not hedge your option position. The cost to you would be the current market price less what you paid for your options (strike price). (Refer to the *Investment Strategies* chapter for further explanation.)

35. What rules apply when the stock received is not freely transferable or is subject to a risk of forfeiture?

(These rules apply to "insider" stock that is not freely transferable under the securities laws, such as under SEC Act of 1934 Section 16(b) or SEC Regulation Section 230.144.)

If the stock is not freely transferable or is subject to a risk of forfeiture, the transaction is not considered closed until these restrictions lapse.

The compensation element is determined when the restrictions lapse. The amount of compensation is the excess of the fair market value of the stock *on that date* over the option price.

If the restrictions will never lapse, the transaction is considered closed and the fair market value of the stock is adjusted to consider the restrictions.

Since this postponement puts a "cloud" of uncertainty over the tax results of the transaction, an election is available to secure the tax results.

36. Should I make gifts of non-qualified options for estate planning? What is the tax impact of doing this?

In some circumstances, it is advantageous to make gifts of non-qualified options or restricted stock. Before going ahead, be sure such transfers are permitted under the terms of the option or the stock restrictions.

Making gifts of these options or stock could have an estate tax advantage of shifting future appreciation to your donee.

Please be aware that gifts of employee stock options that have not vested are considered to be incomplete until the shares are vested. The IRS recently ruled in Revenue Ruling 98-21 that when an employee cannot exercise an option until the employee provides additional services to the employer, the transfer of the option to a donee is not a completed gift until the later of (1) the transfer date or (2) the time when the donee's right to exercise the option is no longer conditioned on the employee's performance of services.

For example, Jill Smith gives non-qualified employee stock options for 300 shares of Tech stock on June 30, 1998. The value of the options on June 30, 1998, is $0. In order for the shares to vest, Jill must work three years after June 30, 1998, at Tech. The gift will not be considered to be complete until June 30, 2001. If the value of the options has increased to $200,000 on June 30, 2001, that will be the value of the completed taxable gift.

It is unclear whether the IRS intends to apply this ruling to transfers before the date the ruling was issued, May 4, 1998.

The election to treat the transfer is completed, and does not apply for gift tax purposes. If the option is exercised and the stock is subject to a risk of forfeiture, the gift still is not a completed gift.

Gifts of a present interest in property (generally, not in trust) of up to $10,000 per year per donee, per donor are exempt from gift tax. Gifts in excess of the $10,000 per year are subject to gift tax.

In most cases, the gift should be substantial to justify the expenses required to value the stock or options for gift tax reporting.

Making these gifts does not eliminate the income tax consequence for the donor. When the donee exercises the option, the donor who originally received the option will still be subject to tax on the ordinary income amount (Ltr Rul 9722022). The tax basis of the donee will be increased for the ordinary income recognized by the donor.

If the donor is deceased at the time the option is exercised, the ordinary income will be taxed to the holder of the option as income with respect of a decedent.

Restricted stock does not receive a "fresh start" basis adjustment like other inherited property.

EIGHT

▼

INVESTMENT STRATEGIES

Holders of low cost basis stock with a concentration of their net worth in a single stock position are faced with the dilemma of how to preserve the value of the stock and create diversification while retaining the rights of ownership. The conventional strategy for realizing stock value is to sell a portion of the holding and reinvest the proceeds in a diversified portfolio. However, the adverse tax implications of selling low cost basis stock may make this strategy undesirable.

The following strategies represent some of the most powerful solutions available to holders of concentrated stock positions who are unwilling to sell their stock. They address freely tradable equity securities only and do not look at the rules and requirements faced by holders of control or restricted securities. These strategies are effective at creating liquidity, diversifying, and hedging stock positions while avoiding some of the drawbacks of an open-market sale. The use of these strategies may cause adverse tax consequences. Prior to entering into any of these strategies, you should consult a qualified tax advisor.

MARGIN

Margining one's account, when done appropriately, can be an effective use of leverage and a viable alternative for raising cash for the purpose of diversification and potentially reducing the risk

STRATEGY	Diversification	Defer Tax	Hedge	Liquidity
No Action		X		
Margin/Borrow Against Stock	X	X		X
Hedge Puts		X	X	
In-the-money-calls	X	X	X	X
Collars		X	X	
Exchange Fund	X	X	X	

of a concentrated position.

The use of margin is a strategy that involves using the underlying stock as collateral for a loan. The shareholder may normally borrow up to 50% of the value of their freely tradable, margin-eligible equity positions. (New and small companies are not always marginable.) The amount of credit extended to the shareholder will vary depending upon the purpose of the loan, the number of shares outstanding, the stock's daily trading volume, and other factors set by the Federal Reserve and the shareholder's chosen brokerage firm.

ADVANTAGES

- **Liquidity**: Proceeds can be used for diversification and potential risk reduction.
- **Retain ownership**: Holder retains ownership and potential appreciation of the stock.
- **Voting and dividend rights**: Holder retains the voting and dividend rights of the shares.
- **Defer capital gains**: Borrowing does not trigger a taxable event on the underlying shares. Please consult with your tax advisor.
- **Potential tax benefits**: The interest expense incurred from the margin loan is generally tax-deductible against an equal amount of income from interest and dividends. The deduction is contingent upon the loan being used for investment

purposes. (The purchase of tax-exempt securities does not qualify.)

DISADVANTAGES

- **Borrowing limits / downside risk**: The maximum credit extended to the shareholder is 50% of the stock value. Thereafter, equity maintenance requirements must be maintained in the account. (Restricted stock may require higher maintenance requirements).
- **Interest expense**: The shareholder pays the borrowing costs. (The interest rate of the loan floats from a set base rate).

PROTECTIVE PUT

A protective put is designed to provide investors with a hedge against a downside movement in a concentrated stock position, while still allowing them to participate in potential gains. When executed correctly, this strategy works as a hedge against the kind of sudden drop that can wipe out your unrealized gains.

Whereas standard stock options (a.k.a. calls) allow you to buy a stock at a specified price, usually in order to realize the upside of a stock's growth, put options allow you to sell the associated stock at a predetermined price by a specified date. A hedge put will protect the investor's stock position below the strike price of the put. Any appreciation in the underlying stock above the cost of protection will be profit for the holder of the put.

ADVANTAGES

- **Realize the upside**: Participate fully in any appreciation of the stock less the cost of the put.
- **Downside protection**: Your net worth is protected within the limits of the put in the event of a market

crash or a severe drop in the underlying stock price.

- **Capital gains deferral**: Under certain circumstances the sale of puts is not considered a sale of the underlying shares by the IRS and may not be subject to capital gains taxes.
- **Voting / dividend rights**: Dividend rights and voting control are maintained.

DISADVANTAGES

- **Cost**: The up-front premium paid for the put can be expensive depending on the stock's volatility and expiration date.
- **Tax treatment**: This transaction may adversely affect the holding period necessary to qualify for long-term capital gains treatment. Please consult your tax advisor on constructive sale rules.

COVERED CALL

Call options are securities that give the holder the right to buy the underlying stock at a specific price by a certain date. Investors who hold low cost basis stock may be concerned about the risk of holding a concentrated stock position. Investors who are in this situation and do not want to sell the shares may consider selling a call option against the shares they hold long. In exchange for granting this right, the seller of the call option will receive a premium. With this premium in hand you now have some downside protection up to the amount of premium received.

ADVANTAGES

- **Income**: The sale of the call gives the seller money in hand.
- **Hedging**: The proceeds from the sale provide

downside protection equal to the amount of the premium received.

- **Dividend / voting rights**: Both dividend and voting rights are retained.

DISADVANTAGES

- **Reduced upside**: Appreciation in the stock is relinquished if the stock price exceeds the strike price of the call.
- **Downside risk**: The value of the stock is still subject to a decline if the drop in the stock price is greater than the call premium received.

IN-THE-MONEY CALLS

Do you ever feel like the poorest millionaire in town? You are worth millions on paper in options, but with all your bills you feel poor. You could sell some stock options, but is there another way to generate cash? Yes.

Investors who hold low cost basis stock may be concerned about the risk of holding a concentrated stock position. Investors who are in this situation and do not want to sell the shares at this time may consider selling an in-the-money call option. In exchange for granting this right, the seller of the call option will receive a premium. This premium will serve to monetize and hedge the value of your shares.

This is how it works. An investor will sell an option that obligates the investor to sell the stock at a specific price (strike price) by expiration. In exchange for giving up the potential upside of the stock above the strike price, the investor receives the option premium. This premium hedges the stock position by the amount received.

In this strategy, when the strike price is below the stock price, the option is considered in-the-money. The premium received can be substantial, thereby providing considerable downside protection for the underlying shares in the event the price declines. Conversely, since the investor has granted the right to have the stock purchased at the strike price, if the stock rallies, the investor will not participate past the strike price.

ADVANTAGES

- **Income**: The sale of the call monetizes the difference between the strike price and the stock's current market price.
- **Hedging**: This strategy hedges a decline in the stock price up to the amount of the premium received.
- **Ownership / voting rights**: Holder maintains ownership of the shares and voting rights.

DISADVANTAGES

- **Reduced upside**: Selling a call limits the upside potential.
- **Downside risk**: The value of the stock is still subject to a decline if the drop in the stock is greater than the call premium received.
- **Tax treatment**: This transaction may terminate the holding period of the underlying shares for long-term capital gains treatment if the shares are held for one year or less. (The one year period may extend to eighteen months.) Please consult your tax advisor.

COLLARS

If you are concerned about the near-term market outlook for your stock and options, it is possible to protect their value while at the same time allowing for some additional participation in the upside.

The simultaneous purchase of a put option and the sale of a

call option is called a collar. The put side of the collar will protect against a decrease in the stock price below the strike price of the put. To finance this protection, a call is sold for the equivalent premium of the cost of the put. In effect, the investor has purchased downside protection on the value of the shares (put) and paid for it by foregoing the potential appreciation above a certain price (call). A collar strategy may be considered a constructive sale, and must be reviewed with your tax advisor prior to entering into the contract.

ADVANTAGES

- **Downside protection**: The value of the stock position is protected if the stock price falls below the put option strike price.
- **Upside appreciation**: The investor participates in the increase in the stock price up to the call option strike price.
- **Minimal expense**: The proceeds from selling the call can be structured to partially or completely offset the cost of purchasing the put.
- **Flexibility**: Options offer flexible maturity date, strike prices and settlement methods.
- **Ownership / voting rights**: Holder retains ownership of the shares and the voting rights.

DISADVANTAGES

- **Reduced upside potential**: The sale of the call option limits the upside potential to the strike price of the call.
- **Tax treatment**: This transaction may terminate the holding period of the underlying shares for long-term capital gains treatment if the shares are held for one year or less. (The one year period may extend to eighteen months.) Please consult with your tax advisor.

EXCHANGE FUND

If you have a multimillion-dollar position, exchange and swap funds can allow you to diversify your position without any immediate tax liability. An exchange fund is an investment vehicle that allows qualified investors with low cost basis stock that is highly appreciated to diversify their holding on a tax-free basis.

People who own significant concentrated stock positions in publicly traded companies often find it hard, both practically and emotionally, to sell a large portion of their shares. Sometimes employees are forbidden from selling their shares during a certain period of time and at other times they may find it hard to liquidate without triggering a widespread market sell-off. The Exchange Fund was designed to allow large stakeholders the ability to diversify their wealth.

Note: During the fall of 1999 there has been speculation that the laws allowing exchange funds might be rescinded. Please speak with your financial advisor to check if this alternative investment is still available.

ADVANTAGES

- **Diversification**: Allows investors to diversify holdings into at least 50-100 different stocks without realizing current capital gains.
- **Tax-free exchange**: Diversification is attained without triggering any immediate tax liabilities.

DISADVANTAGES

- **High minimum**: These funds generally require a minimum investment of $500,000 to $1,000,000, and a liquid net worth of $5,000,000 to participate.
- **Long-term commitment**: Securities deposited in an exchange fund are normally intended to be five to ten year investments.

OVER-THE-COUNTER (OTC) OPTIONS

Several of these strategies utilize over-the-counter (OTC) options. OTC options, unlike standardized options that are listed on an exchange, are customized by brokerage firms to meet specific investor requirements. The terms of these options, such as the expiration dates, strike prices and settlement methods can all be customized to meet an investor's unique financial requirements. OTC options are useful when writing calls because they can be designed as European-style, ensuring that they are not called away early.

The effectiveness of each of the strategies revolves around your individual tax situation. Events such as holding periods for stock ownership, new tax laws, and the intricacies of the alternative minimum tax make for a confusing array of variables that affect your investment planning. In the end, there is no substitution for a good tax advisor and financial consultant who specializes in custom options-oriented strategies.

CONCLUSION

▼

We felt compelled, both personally and professionally, to write this book. We have watched far too many people with paper fortunes lose everything. Most of their lives were irrevocably damaged by their mistakes. Yet, the real tragedy is that most of their losses were unnecessary. These people were not uneducated, they simply did not take the right steps. They let bad planning and emotional decision-making dictate their futures.

We watched a friend, a very bright and talented woman who worked for a software company, receive a large grant of company stock options. The stock was trading at $10 and quickly rose to $74. She and her husband were ecstatic. Finally, she was an optionaire! She became pregnant, and they started looking for a larger house in Silicon Valley. It seemed that their dreams were coming true. Unfortunately, she allowed emotion to interfere with financial planning. We cannot stress strongly enough: Never allow emotional attachment and feeling towards your company stock to dictate your financial planning.

You know what comes next. The company started having problems; the stock sank back to $10 per share. Our friends lost all their paper net worth.

Now, this is not a riches-to-rags story. It's just not a riches-to-riches story. Our friends live an hour from the city. He commutes and she is raising her child at home. They were wonderful people before all this, and they still are. However, they did not end up with their dreams. They lost millions. And they discovered the painful truth that incredible opportunities sometimes appear only once.

The part of this story that is most distressing is that it never had to end that way. If they had planned correctly . . . if they had had hedged and diversified their position . . . if they had gotten the right kind of tax advice . . . things would have been different.

There are simply too many stories like this: hot young executives who thought they were invincible, software engineers or IT managers who forgot to apply their mathematical expertise to financial planning, employees of all stripes who put company loyalty before common sense.

Receiving company stock options is no guarantee of lasting wealth. It is not the lottery. It requires some effort on your part. But the work involved is not nearly as hard as your job. It is more like doing your taxes . . . only this time, you get to keep the money.

You can control many of the potential threats to your fortune—if you take the right steps.

ESSENTIAL STEPS FOR OPTIONAIRES
(Four Golden Rules for Keeping Your Gold)

1. Educate yourself.

Reading this book is a great start. You should also consult your stock plan administrator or your company's financial officer, who can give you information on your company stock options and employee stock purchase plan. The information should include all the relevant company and SEC rules and regulations and tax consequences.

2. Develop a personal financial plan.

Planning is a crucial prerequisite to all realistic financial strategies for wealth preservation. Don't just guess—plan. Do the work as meticulously as you can. Give serious consideration to creating your plan with a qualified financial advisor.

3. Don't forget the tax consequences.

While tax considerations should never be your primary consideration in financial planning, they are a close second in developing strategies to preserve and maximize your wealth.

Taxes are all too often the downfall of optionaires. Be sure to consult with a tax advisor experienced in the tax consequences of company stock and options.

4.   Get the best help you can find.

Unless you are absolutely convinced of your own omniscience, find a financial advisor highly experienced in employee stock options. After all, you are a millionaire on paper, so you might as well do what other millionaires do: hire good help. On your way to finding the right financial advisor, here are some questions you should ask prospective advisors, and other considerations to bear in mind:

QUESTIONS TO ASK A FINANCIAL ADVISOR

1.   What is their level of experience and training with employee stock options?

We have found that the vast majority of financial advisors today have received little education or training pertaining to employee stock options. Ask your advisor about their level of training in this area.

2.   Do they spend the majority of their time working with clients who have employee options and concentrated company stock?

The rules and regulations relating to employee stock options and concentrated stock positions change frequently. If your advisor does not spend the majority of their time focusing on the applicable rules, it would be challenging, if not impossible, for them to stay current.

3.   What are the financial strength and resources of the advisor's firm?

Does their firm have an Option Strategy Department,

Executive Financial Services Department, Restricted Stock Department and Alternate Investments Group? A common misperception is that a small firm will provide a higher degree of service. We have found that service is more closely associated with your individual advisor than with the size of the firm. With regard to financial services and investment resources, typically the larger and more established firms offer a wider array of alternatives and access to many of the most desirable financial instruments.

4.   Does the advisor prepare a financial plan and review it with each client annually?

Writing and maintaining a financial plan and reviewing it annually should be required from your advisor.

5.   Is estate planning a major component of the advisors planning services?

All optionaires have the need for estate planning. Estate planning involves generation wealth transfer and related taxes due upon death. It is easy to overlook this issue, but the sooner you start planning and transferring assets outside of your estate, the less your future tax liability will be. It is critical that your advisor be as knowledgeable about estate planning as about option planning.

OTHER CONSIDERATIONS

1.   Fee-based management v. commissions and transaction costs:

There are two differing fee structures that financial advisors use, transactional-based commissions and fee-based management. Transactional advisors are "old school," charging a commission for each transaction, and have no financial incentive to grow your account. Their incentive is to trade your account; the more trades they make, the more revenue they generate, regardless of whether you make money or not. In recent years, advisors have started to shift to fee-based management, charging a flat percentage for assets under management and not charging commissions or transactional costs. This style of advising eliminates the potential "conflict of interest" that can exist between transactional advisors and their clients. We feel that fee-based management represents your interests better than transactional advising.

2. Level of personal trust:

Study after study has shown that the top reason given for choosing an advisor is trust. Ask your potential advisor for references. Spend time on your due diligence and take the time to get to know the advisor's investment philosophy. Your overall impression of the financial services firm you choose will come down to the individual financial advisor you work with more than any other factor. So, your choice of advisor is more important than your choice of firm.

3. Fees charged by the advisor—are they worth it?

Everyone wants a good deal and no one wants to overpay. Sure, you can invest in a no load index fund and have a management fee that is less than a half of one percent annually, or you can choose to work with an advisor who charges one to three percent annually. Is an advisor worth it? What do you get for your money? An advisor who adequately answers the questions listed above, works under a fee-based management system, holds individual stocks within your portfolio and assists you with estate and tax planning can be a cost saver.

Performance, access to special alternative investments, personalized option strategies, and tax efficient planning can more than cover the advisory fee. A good financial advisor, much like a good CPA, should cover their fees with their performance and ideas.

4. Investment team or sole practitioner?

The growing trend for high net worth clients is to have an investment management team rather than a sole practitioner. The team approach gives you access to several advisors within one group who have different areas of expertise. Team members are always available and there are no issues with your advisor being away for two weeks on vacation. We see no reason to choose a sole practitioner over a team.

5. Number of clients?

Everyone wants to hire an advisor who is successful, but your advisor might be too successful at getting new clients. Many advisors who have been in the industry for years have several hundred—or even several thousand—clients. Do you want to be one of thousands? The more elite management teams limit their number of clients, and we agree that this is in your best interest. If possible, look for an advisory team who limits its clientele to one hundred or less per team member.

We have given a lot of thought to why some optionaires take the last steps to real success, while others become mired in denial, feelings of false security, and confused loyalties. Of course, we are not psychologists, but we have noticed that our most successful clients treat financial planning, and the use of the strategic approaches described in this book, as a natural extension of their jobs. They worked hard to create their fortunes, and they find it natural to work hard to preserve them or hire someone to do it for them. They know that the last few steps to security and lasting wealth are no different than the first: carefully considered actions that must be taken boldly to ensure success. And they know that no one can take the last steps but themselves.

It has taken an extraordinary effort for you to become an optionaire. Don't stop now. Don't allow all your previous efforts to be wasted. We urge you to take the actions necessary to translate your paper fortune into lasting wealth.

The next steps are up to you. We wish you all the continued success in the world.

DEFINITIONS
▼

Alternative Minimum Tax (AMT)
The alternative minimum tax rates are 26% for the first $175,000 of alternative minimum taxable income (AMTI) and 28% for AMTI over $175,000. The maximum rates as described above for the regular tax for sales of capital assets on or after January 1, 1998, will also apply for the alternative minimum tax. Single persons have an AMT exemption of $33,750, phased out by 25% of the excess of AMTI over $112,500, and eliminated for AMTI of $247,500 or more. The AMT exemption on a joint return for married persons is $45,000, phased out by 25% of the excess of AMTI over $150,000, and eliminated for AMTI of $330,000 or more.

The Federal income tax is actually a parallel tax system. There is a "regular" tax that most of us are fairly familiar with. There is also an AMT. The tax is computed using both methods, and you generally pay the higher tax. If the ATM does apply, a portion of the excess over the regular tax may be available as a tax credit in a later year, treated somewhat like a prepayment of the later year's tax.

American-style Option
An option that may be exercised at any time between the purchase date and expiration date of the option contract. Most exchange-traded, equity options are American-style.

Assignment
When the writer of an option contract receives an exercise notice that requires them to buy (in the case of a put) or sell (in the case of a call) the underlying security at the designated strike price.

At-the-money Option
Options are "at-the-money" when the exercise price is equal to the current market price of the underlying security. For example, an

employee is given 100 employee stock options of XYZ Company with an exercise price of $10 per share. The options are at-the-money when XYZ Company's current market value is also $10 per share.

Bearish
A common term used by investors to mean that they lack confidence in an investment.

Blackout Period
A period of time in which securities law restricts the sale of a particular stock. Two common times when blackout periods occur: during the first 180 days of a newly formed public company and around the time of earnings releases.

Bullish
A common term used by investors to mean that they are positive on an investment.

Call
An option contract that allows the holder to purchase the underlying security at a specified price during a fixed period of time until expiration.

Cashless Exercise
An exercise strategy in which employee stock options are simultaneously exercised and sold for the net cash proceeds (gain - taxes - transaction costs = net proceeds).

Closing Purchase
Purchase of a listed or OTC option contract to eliminate or undo an existing short option position.

Closing sale
Sale of a listed or OTC option contract to eliminate or reduce an existing long option position.

Collar
A derivative strategy that can be used to lock in the gains of an existing long position at a specified price during a fixed period of time. Collars are created when an investor buys a put option and writes a call option against the same underlying security. While this strategy eliminates downside risk on the position, it also reduces upside potential. For a further explanation see *Investment Strategy* chapter.

Constructive Sale
When a security is deemed to have undergone a taxable event even though it has not been sold. This can happen when an investor uses other investment vehicles to secure the current share price within a narrow range effectively locking in the current price.

Cost Basis
The original cost paid for a security.

Covered option writing
Strategy in which an individual writes, or sells, calls against an equal long position in the underlying security or sells, or writes, puts against an equal short position in the underlying security.

Crossover Point
The point where alternative minimum taxable income (AMTI) liability is equal to your ordinary income tax liability.

Derivative Security
A security whose value is primarily derived from the value of another security.

Disqualifying Disposition
A disqualifying disposition is created when an ISO acquired stock is sold within two years of the option grant date one year from the exercise date. This transaction is taxed as ordinary income.

Diversification
When additional investments are added to a portfolio. This is done in an attempt to reduce risk and/or increase performance.

Employee Stock Option
An option, granted from the employer to the employee, to purchase company stock at a specified strike price during a fixed period of time.

Employee Stock Purchase Plan (ESPP)
An investment offered by an employer to the employees in which they can buy company stock. Normally the employer discounts the price of the company share price.

European-style Options
An option contract that may only be exercised on a specific date (typically on the day before expiration). Non-equity options generally trade European-style.

Exchange Fund
An investment vehicle that is designed to provide investors with tax-free diversification. It is intended for investors who hold a large amount of one stock, normally $500,000 to $1,000,000 or more.

Exercise
When the holder of employee stock options carries out the right to purchase or sell the underlying security.

Exercise Price / Grant Price / Option Price / Strike Price
The price at which the holder of employee stock options is entitled to buy the underlying company stock.

Exercise and Hold
When an option is exercised and the individual retains ownership

of the granted option. After an exercise and hold transaction, the security is long.

An exercise and hold strategy is commonly used to take advantage of potential tax benefits involving ISOs. When using this strategy, the optionaire will exercise and hold the underlying security.

Exercise and Sell
When the optionee exercises the stock options (ISOs or NQSOs), the underlying security is immediately sold. The optionee receives the proceeds of the sale minus ordinary income tax withholdings and the cost of the exercise, which generally includes administrative costs.

Exercise and Sell to Cover
The optionee sells a portion of the employee stock options to cover exercise costs, and the remaining shares from the exercise are held long.

Expiration Date
The expiration date is the date on which the right to exercise an employee's stock options expires. All vested, non-exercised options will be lost after the expiration date.

Expiration Time
The time of day on the expiration date by which an option contract must be exercised before the contract is deemed worthless.

Future Value
The value in tomorrow's dollars adjusted for inflation.

Good Until Cancelled (Order)
When an order is placed with a brokerage and is intended to stay as an open order until cancelled.

Grant (See **Option Grant**)

Grant Date
The specific day on which employee stock options are granted to the employee by the employer.

Grant Price (See **Exercise Price**)

Hedge
A strategy used to reduce downside risk by offsetting the existing position with another transaction. A common example of a hedge strategy is a "hedge put."

Holder
An individual who holds a security. Also refers to the purchaser of a call or put option.

Holding Period
Period of time between the purchase date and sale date of a security.

Initial Public Offering (IPO)
The first time a company offers its shares for sale to the public on the open market.

Incentive Stock Option (ISO)
A type of employee stock option that qualifies for preferential tax treatment provided all requirements are followed.

In-the-money
An option is "in-the-money" if the underlying security is trading at a higher price than the exercise price of the option. For example, XYZ stock is trading at $40 when the exercise price of the option is $35. The option is $5 in-the-money.

Intrinsic value
The portion of a listed option premium that derives its price from the amount by which an option is in-the-money.

Life of Grant
Period of time during which options may be exercised.

Liquidity
Refers to the level of ease with which an asset can be converted into cash.

Long position
A long position is created when an investor purchases a security that is not offset by a short position. For example, an investor who buys 100 shares of XYZ Company has created a long position of 100 shares, or is long 100 shares.

Long-Term Capital Gains Tax
Under current tax law, when a security is purchased and held for twelve months or more, it qualifies for long-term capital gains. Currently, the long-term capital gains tax rate is 20%.

Margin Account
A brokerage account that allows an investor to purchase securities on credit borrowed against securities held long in the account. Margin is subject to margin requirements and rules established by the Federal Reserve and by the firm carrying the account. Interest is charged on the money that is borrowed or margined.

Margin Call
When the brokerage firm that has lent an investor demands additional monies or securities in a margin account due to the increase in the debit balance which is above the maximum level.

Non-Qualified Stock Option (NQSO or NQ)
A type of employee stock option that is taxable as ordinary income at the time of exercise. Unlike ISOs, NQSOs do not qualify for favorable tax treatment.

Open Order
An order that has been placed but has not been executed. For example, an order is placed to sell 1000 shares of XYZ at $55 per share. The stock is currently trading at $53 per share. Until the stock hits $55 per share or higher, it will not be sold and will remain an open order.

Opportunity Cost
The alternate use of cash. As related to employee stock options, opportunity cost is the loss of interest or growth that might have been earned on money used to exercise options.

Optionaire
An individual who has accumulated substantial wealth through company stock and options.

Optionee
A holder of employee stock options.

Option Grant
An Option Grant refers to a specific group of employee stock options, ISOs or NQSOs, that are given to the employee by the employer. Grants are identified by their unique grant numbers. When exercising employee stock options, it is essential that you inform the exercise administrator which grant of options are to be exercised.

Option Price (See Exercise Price)

Option Type
Refers to classification of an option contract (call or put).

Out-of-the-money
An option is "out-of-the-money" if the underlying security is trading at a lower price than the exercise price of the option. For example, XYZ stock is trading at $40 when the exercise price of the option is $45.

Premium
The cost of a listed or OTC traded option contract. Premium is paid by the option buyer and received by the option writer. For example, if you write calls against your existing long position at a cost of $5 per share, you receive a premium of $5 per share.

Present Value
The value in today's dollars of one or more payments to be received in the future.

Put
An option contract that allows the holder of the contract to sell the underlying security at a set price for a fixed period of time.

Qualifying Disposition
A qualifying disposition is created when an optionaire holds ISO acquired stock for a minimum period of two years from the grant date and one year from the exercise date. Consequently, option earnings can receive preferential tax treatment.

Short Position
A short position is created when an investor sells a security that they do not own. For example, an investor who sells 100 shares of XYZ Company that he does not already own has created a short position of 100 shares, or is short 100 shares.

Short-Term Capital Gains Tax

Under current tax law, when a security is sold within 12 months of its purchase date, it is considered a short-term capital gain. The gain or loss is taxed as ordinary income tax.

Strike Price (See Exercise Price)

Time Value

The portion of a listed option premium that derives its price from the amount of time that remains until the option contract expires.

Uncovered Option Writing

Generally considered an aggressive strategy in which an investor writes call or put options without owning the underlying security.

Underlying Security

The security that the option bases its value upon.

Vested Options

Vested options are options that have passed the required holding period, and can be exercised.

Vesting Date

The date on which your options become available to exercise.

Volatility

The amount of price movement a security experiences, normally expressed as a percentage.

Writer

The seller of an option contract.

APPENDIX

▼

EMOTIONAL INTELLIGENCE QUIZ

1. Have you ever felt that your company stock and option position was safe enough for you to ignore it for a period of time?
2. Have you ever felt that your stock and options were such a tremendous responsibility that you would rather just not think about them?
3. Have your company stock and options ever given you a feeling of power and/or invulnerability?
4. Has a dip in the price of your company stock ever made you feel depressed?
5. Do you feel comforted by your options?
6. Do you ever feel that your options look out for you?

If you answered yes to one or more of these questions, then it is likely that your financial decisions are somewhat distorted by emotion. A lack of objectivity in financial planning by optionaires usually leads to two kinds of crucial mistakes:

1. waiting too long to exercise options, with negative price and tax consequences
2. deciding to exercise based solely on tax consequences rather than on a combination of market conditions and tax consequences

Both of these mistakes can be disastrous. We recommend that anyone who has ever made emotional decisions about finance re-examine their attitudes towards their company stock and options. Be as honest and objective as possible. Imagine that the stock and options positions are not really yours, and that you are merely giving advice to someone else on preserving and growing their wealth.

OPTIONAIRE OBJECTIVITY QUIZ

1. Why am I holding a sizable percentage of my liquid assets in one investment?
2. Why do I feel my company will out-perform the broader market and the other companies within my industry?
3. Why do I feel my company will grow faster than our competitors' stock?
4. My peers, in the same financial situation, are also holding the bulk of their company options; do they know something I don't? What if their overweighting in their companies is correct and I'm wrong? What will happen to them if time demonstrates that I was right? What will happen to me if they are right?
5. Do I ever plan on selling a sizable percent of my company stock? When? Why then? Why not now?
6. How much money do I need? By when? How did I come to this amount?
7. What formula have I used to determine my tolerance to risk? Did I use a formula or did I just wing it?

Review your answers, be critical, and review them with your friends and family. If they feel that you are being too emotional, then you probably are and should seek the assistance of a financial advisor.

Your options do not require your love, but they do require your attention. We would never tell you that you are wrong about the outlook for your company's market performance. But we urge you to ask yourself, what if you are wrong? If you diversify your investment portfolio and your company stock continues to rise, you will not fully participate in the upside, but your portfolio should have less risk. However, if you are wrong and the price goes down, you may have only a fraction of the wealth you have today. Can you afford to lose the net worth you have vested in your options? We see it happen every day, and we can tell you objectively that the prudent step is almost always to diversify or hedge your position.

The first part of successful financial planning for the optionaire lies in objectivity about investing. The second part lies in objectivity about personal needs. Decisions are based on targeting objectives, and goals are based on needs.

STOCK OPTION PLANNING WORKSHEET

| Name: | | Stock: | | Date: | | Current Price: | |

Non-vested Options:

Option Type (ISO/NQ)	Number of Shares	Grant Date	Vesting Date	Expiration Date	Strike Price/Cost	Market Value	Cost to Buy/Exercise	Pre Tax Value
						$	$	$
						$	$	$
						$	$	$
Total						$	$	$

Vested Options (Not Yet Exercised)

Option Type (ISO/NQ)	Number of Shares	Grant Date	Vesting Date	Expiration Date	Strike Price/Cost	Market Value	Cost to Buy/Exercise	Pre Tax Value
			n/a			$	$	$
			n/a			$	$	$
			n/a			$	$	$
Total			n/a			$	$	$

Exercised and Held Options and/or Shares Held Long:

Option Type(ISO/NQ) or Stock	Number of Shares	Grant Date	Grant Price	Exercised Date	Exercised Price	Market Value	Shares Held at (Brokerage Firm)
							$
							$
							$
Total							$

Exercised and Sold Options and/or Shares Sold:

Option Type(ISO/NQ) or Stock	Number of Shares	Grant Date	Grant Price	Exercised Date	Exercised Price	Date Sold	Sale Price Value at Date of Sale	Shares Sold at (Brokerage Firm)
							$	
							$	
							$	
Total							$	

If you would like a complimentary copy of this worksheet on Excel, please email us at StillmanPublishing@hotmail.com

ABOUT THE AUTHORS

GABRIEL FENTON & JOSEPH S. STERN, III

Recognized nationally as innovators in strategic planning for Employee Stock Options and concentrated stock positions, Gabriel Fenton and Joseph S. Stern, III are senior partners for a Corporate Service Employee Stock Option group with a major Wall Street firm.

As Portfolio Managers and Financial Advisors, Gabriel and Joseph's primary focus is to address the wealth management needs of the founders and senior management of leading technology companies.

Gabriel Fenton has been providing investment advice for over ten years. His emphasis is on building strategies to reduce concentrated stock and option positions and also estate planning. Gabriel is securities licensed on both coasts and maintains his Series 6, 7, 63 and 65 licenses.

Joseph Stern focuses on building hedging and diversification strategies for individuals with highly concentrated equity positions. He seeks to build wealth for his clients through the use of alternative investments, such as derivatives, private placements and exchange funds. Joseph maintains his Series 7, 31, 63 and 65 securities licenses.

You may reach them at: G_Fenton@hotmail.com
or Joseph_Stern3@hotmail.com

MICHAEL C. GRAY, CPA

Michael C. Gray founded his CPA firm, Michael Gray, CPA, October 1, 1996. Mike has been a CPA in California since March 1977. He received his BS in accounting and MBA at San Jose State University in June 1974 and June 1978, respectively. He is a past chairman of the tax committee for the San Jose CPAs and past member of the state tax committee for the California CPAs. He is also a member of the Santa Clara County Estate Planning Council, and is a lay member of the Santa Clara County Bar Association. Mike works with many people on tax planning for incentive stock options and non-qualified stock options.

You can contact Mike at mgray@taxtrimmers.com or visit his web site at www.taxtrimmers.com

MORE HELP FOR READERS

How can you keep up to date on tax developments for employee stock options?

As the most significant source of new wealth in the United States, employee stock options will be the focus of continuing tax developments—including IRS rulings, court rulings and legislation.

How can you keep up with these developments?

Subscribe to a free email newsletter by Michael Gray, CPA: *Michael Gray, CPA's Bottom Line!*

To subscribe, just visit the web site for Michael Gray, CPA – www.taxtrimmers.com. You'll find the registration form on the home page.

You will also find www.taxtrimmers.com to be an excellent resource of past newsletters, articles and answers to frequently asked questions.

Would your company like to educate its employees about tax rules for employee stock options?

Michael Gray, CPA, is available for a limited number of presentations to employee groups about the tax rules for employee stock options and stock purchase plans. For more information, call (408) 918-3166 or write Michael Gray, CPA, 1265 S. Bascom Ave., Ste. 106, San Jose, CA 95128-3533.

ORDER YOUR COPY TODAY

Fax orders: (520) 833-8374

On-line orders: Stillmanpublishing@hotmail.com

PRICE *($39.95 US)* _____ NO. COPIES   SUBTOTAL _____

Shipping: *$4.00 for the first book and $2.00 for each additional book:* _____

Tax: (California Residents add applicable sales tax): _____

TOTAL: _____

Payment: ❑ Cheque   ❑ Credit Card

❑ VISA   ❑ Master Card   ❑ Optima   ❑ AMEX   ❑ Discover

Card number: _____

Name on card: _____

Expiration date: ___ / ___

Signature: _____

Shipping address: _____

City _____ State ____ Zip _____

Email _____